The thing's you

DON'T

know that you

DON'T

know.

The thing's you
DON'T
know that you
DON'T
know.

Written by,

Harland Williams

ISBN 978-0-557-18222-0

Dedicated to Walter Strasser - Just keeping my promise!

Table of Contents

DID YOU KNOW??

FOREWORD

DID YOU KNOW?

How often have you heard that question in your lifetime?

Did you know? We hear it all the time. "Did you know that the human body is 85% water? Did you know that pigs are smarter than dogs? Did you know that if a mini van dropped on your head it can kill you, or a least reshape your body? Did you know that people with no arms use their nubs to make chicken pot pie shells?" Ok, I made that one up but it's probably true.

Anyway, there's all kinds of facts out there, most of them pretty obvious. You've heard them, giraffes are the tallest animals, Everest is the highest mountain, humans are the most intelligent creatures... but, are we?

As it turns out maybe we're not. What if I told you there's a whole bunch of things that you *don't* know? Everyday things? Things that are right under our noses. I know it sounds impossible, but I assure you that this book is going to uncover some startling facts, concepts and ideas. This book is going to reveal to you hundreds of things you *should* know but probably don't. Everyday things that need to be talked about and brought out into the open. Things that for whatever reason remain overlooked or ignored, tucked away or forgotten. Be warned that some of these findings will be revelations. Some of you reading may be shocked, stunned or even horrified. Some of you may have your whole belief system shaken up, rearranged, or worse, enlightened. Some of you may need chin surgery after your jaw drops from absorbing the startling information you are about to read. Just so you know, repeated jaw drops could lead to severe jaw damage. A dysfunctional jaw could lead to starvation and the inability to ask for food. A damaged jaw will prevent you from forming coherent words and sentences. I urge you to read the following pages slowly and carefully and if needs be, wear a hockey helmet with the chinstrap securely in place. You are about to discover there are a whole plethera of things you *don't know, you don't know.*

Sometimes it is not easy to accrue new data, to absorb new information, to stuff more stuff into our already crowded brains. Let us not forget we live in a fast paced world where we believe we pretty much have all the facts we need either in our heads or just a mouse click away on our computers.

Well, prepare to be surprised, even startled. But best of all, prepare to be in the know, as I reveal some of life's most obvious and overlooked didyouknowisms.

Did you know that I just made up the word '*diyouknowisms*'?

Did you know that you already bought this book and you can't take it back?

Did you know that rubber comes from trees and that when they are chopped down they bounce right back up?

Did you know that I know exactly what you're about to do next? Well, I do, watch.

Did you know you're about to turn to the next page?

PART ONE

CHAPTER ONE

The first chapter

See, you turned the page! How did I know? I don't know, I just somehow knew. I somehow see things that others don't. Call it a gift, a calling, a birth defect, whatever. It's time to stop talking about the how's and the why's and just jump right in. Enough of the introspective and the esoteric, let's push forward and start getting you to the juicy new tidbits that are going to stimulate and rejuvenate your life, mind, and powers of the brain.

DID YOU KNOW THAT PUMPKINS ARE THE ONLY LIVING ORGANISMS WITH TRIANGLE EYES?

It's true! Nowhere else in nature do you see a living organism with eyes shaped as triangles. Pumpkins are the only ones. There is no fish, bird or mammal that has the three pointed eyes of the pumpkin. There are no other fruits or vegetables that even have eyes at all, except for the potato, but as far as I know potatoes have horrible eyesight and can be captured quite easily in open fields where they congregate. Pumpkins on the other hand have dark, hallow eyes that they use primarily for sinister activities and their persuit of evil.

Pumpkins wait patiently all year, lying low in subdued pumpkin patches, that is until Halloween night rolls around. It is then, on the scariest of nights, that the lowly pumpkin transforms from the docile, orange, mellons that they are and reveal their pointy, demonic, eyes. Unbelievably, they use these eyes to terrorize small children who are on the prowl for candy. Striking fear into their little hearts as they innocently approach homes looking for a treat.

Sadly, it is near impossible to stop the pumpkins evil, even if it means assaulting the pumpkin. For example, if you were to attack a pumpkin with two isosceles triangles and stab them into it's eyes, people would just think the pumpkin was wearing glasses.

Pumpkins are also the only living organism with lit candles in their heads. Have you ever seen a candle in your golden retriever's head? Your sister's head? Your grandmother's head? I should think not. Only a deviant as evil the pumpkin could even come up with such a demonic way of adding another layer of fright.

But, as strange and as evil as pumpkins are, they can be delicious in the form of a nice pie. They are at their tastiest if you first make the effort to have a certified priest perform an exorcism on your pumpkins and vanquish all the evil prior to making them into a pie. Now all that's left to do is add whip cream, and enjoy a delicious gingery tasting slice of evil.

PRESTO ! !

There, do you see how this works? Do you see what I mean? How you really hadn't tallied all the facts about something as simple as a pumpkin. An object you've had around you your whole life and yet you didn't really take the time to know all there is to know about them. I know, it's embarrassing.

What if you were in a heated conversation about pumpkins and you were missing this essential information? Talk about a social fowpaw.

Well, no more need to worry. As we continue on, you will gain all the knowledge you need to outshine and outsmart all your friends and colleague.

You may never again be the one in a debate or a discussion feeling on the outside, not in the know, worried that the focus turns to you and you're just standing there looking like a drooling dumbass.

By the time you finish this book you are going to shine. You will be the answer person. You will be the voice in the crowd that chimes, "Did you know…"

DID YOU KNOW THAT RHINOCEROSES ARE JUST BIG, FAT, WHITE TRASH, UNICORNS?

Think about it. All animals evolve. They all started as one thing and evolved into what they are today. Unicorns are no different. They were the supermodels of the animal kingdom. Strong, muscular, statuesque, seductive even. They had sexy flowing manes and were hands down undeniably gorgeous. So, where did they go? What happened to them?

To answer that question one needs to draw a parallel to a lot of the hot women we see in society today. As we know "most" Gorgeous women get spoiled. Thing's in life get handed to them, this in turn makes them lazy, and when you're lazy you start to grow old and wrinkly and fat. Boom, thus the fate of the majestic unicorn.

The mystical unicorn stood around in the pine trees and by the mist of waterfalls, up on scenic ridges and at the ends of rainbows. To sum it up they pretty much did a hell of a lot of posing.

Well, how many calories does posing burn? Next to none. So, over the years the lazy ass sons of bitches unicorns started evolving.

They started packing on the pounds and began morphing into what they are known as today, rhinoceros.

It's easy to see because they still have the identifiable trademark horn sticking out of the front of their faces. But long gone are the stunning good looks, splendid white fur and manicured hoofs. Now days the fat, white trash creatures are grey and frumpy, hairless and covered with bumps, warts and fat rolls.

Let their demise be a lesson to all of us that vanity can destroy lives and that a healthy diet and regular exercise are key to retaining our youthful looks.

We can only shake our heads with pity every time we see fairy dust in the air and hear pan flutes playing in the background. For it is these things we automatically associate with the once glamorous unicorn. A once mighty icon of all that is beautiful, but sadly, is now wallowing in a dirty pond in Africa. Its leathery skin caked in rancid mud and zebra feces.

DID YOU KNOW THAT THE 13TH FLOOR IS ON THE 14TH FLOOR

We've all been in an elevator. Many elevators have no button for the 13th floor, why? Superstition they say. Does that mean I can't have a black cat in an elevator? I can't break a mirror in an elevator? Walk under a ladder in an elevator? Stomp the guts out of a daddy long legs in an elevator? So where did the 13th floor go?

I did some investigating and discovered that it's there, right there on the 14th floor.

If you count the floors as you ride up in an elevator, thirteen comes just as the button for the fourteenth floor illuminates. As the elevator doors open you will see the 13th floor on the 14th floor.

I know it's confusing, like an empty space in time, a wormhole, or a void. As the doors open to this ambiguous floor you almost expect to see Michael J. Fox standing there with a Time Flux Capacitor in his hand.

In reality, the 13th floor does exist.

It's the very top floor of buildings with no thirteenth floor that doesn't. Technically if you are in a building that has twenty-three floors but the elevator skips the thirteenth, that means the elevator shows a button for a twenty fourth floor. A floor that truly doesn't exist. If you go to that floor the elevator will open and you will step out into empty, blue sky and plummet twenty three floors until you make contact with the cold pavement far below. What a way to die. Maybe thirteen really is unlucky.

DID YOU KNOW THAT ORANGE IS THE ONLY COLOR YOU CAN EAT?

How did orange get to be an important part of a healthy diet? How is it we can eat orange? We can't eat red or purple or blue or magenta! But how is it that orange grows on trees. In groves? On plantations? How is it that we can mash orange up into a liquid and drink it along with a fine traditional breakfast? I've never had a tall refreshing glass of pink or brown, have you? I've never had to remove seeds or pulp from yellow or green. I've never had to digest navy blue or gold to help stave off scurvy. Ask anybody you know what color an orange is? They all have the same answer, it's orange. There you go! No other color offers such high concentrations of vitamin C. In fact I know of no other color on earth that even comes close to help one get over the common cold. Silver or turquoise has never helped me cure the sniffles. So enjoy orange at least three times a week. Add color to your diet for a happy healthy life.

DID YOU KNOW THAT SOUP IS JUST OLD PEOPLE'S BATH WATER?

Ever go to the grocery store? Sure you have. There are a lot of cans of soup at the grocery store. Humans love soup. We ingest millions of gallons of soup every year, maybe even billions or trillions of gallons. So where does it all come from? How could we possibly come up with so much soup? The answer lies within the answer to another probing question. Where does old people's bath water go to? We live in a highly populated world you and I, over 6 billon and growing. Over 800,000 humans a month pass the age of 65. That's a lot of seniors.

Well, what do we know about seniors? They love to stroll, stare glassy eyed off into space, tremble, make funny grumbling noises, and above all else they love to take baths. The combination of their old, softened skin mixed with the thousands of skin flakes that separate from their bodies and float around the tub make the perfect ingredients for a nice, warm broth.

Over sixty-five years of living and moving and being exposed to the elements make their bodies rich with nutrients and all the flavorings of a cured meat. As they sit naked in the soothing warm bathwater, their flesh releases salts, oils, scabs, crust and a multitude of other flavors that permeate the water and form the foundation to all the delicious soups we've grown to love. After all, to flush all their trillions of gallons of bathwater down the drain would be irresponsible and overwhelm a sewage system that already has far too many demands on it.

The truth is that old people collect their used bath water in cans supplied by the soup companies and fill these containers with their human froth as they splash and play. The end result is delicious soups in a wide myriad of delectable flavors. I recommend the cream of mushroom. The little chunks of grayish mushroom are quite tasty and not really bits of mushroom. Enjoy with a grilled cheese sandwich and Saltine crackers.

EUREKA ! ! !

Okay, are you starting to see how this works? Are you realizing yet just how blind you have been? Do you feel ignorant and ashamed? Look, don't feel bad. Everybody reading this book is having the same reaction. Graduates from Yale and Perdue, M.I.T and Harvard, people from high school, middle school, Mensa, NASA, Montessori, the list goes on and on. Steven Hawking, Albert Einstein, Andy Gibb... they've all overlooked this stuff. It's not easy. Sometimes you just can't see the forest through the trees. Sometimes it's the most obvious stuff that gets overlooked in our lives.

How many times have you spent hours looking for your house keys and then finally you find them hanging in the front door? This book is not here to humiliate you, it's here to enlighten.

Life is too short to be misinformed. Knowledge is power and the Future is a floor wax Made by Johnson & Johnson, around $14 for a 27oz bottle, if you're interested. So let's not be discouraged and let's keep going. This will all pay off in the end when you walk around with more confidence and charisma, knowing that deep inside that brain of yours are valuable nuggets of knowledge.

.

CHAPTER Two

Opening the brain

Believe it or not we live in a world where we have too much information. In fact so much information that we end up missing out on important information. We tend to open our receptors to the stuff on the surface, the stuff that comes from the talking heads in the media, the headlines in the newspapers and magazines. Sure, why not, it's easier that way right? Less taxing, less traumatic. Our brains work hard enough dealing with our everyday lives, why push them harder?

Why? I'll tell you why, because you can. If you walk up to the all you can eat buffet you're going to take a little something of everything. Who goes up to a buffet and just takes one pea, one pork chop, one crab leg. Open your brain the same way you like to open your mouth and stuff it. Take the items beyond the headlines and stuff them into that 'all you can think' brain of yours, C'mon, unlike the all you can eat buffet for $14.99, stuffing your brain is free. So let's keep going, enter some more data into your 'all you can think cranium.'

DID YOU KNOW THAT MANATEES ARE JUST WALRUSES THAT DIDN'T LIKE THE COLD, SO THEY SWAM TO FLORIDA AND GOT THEIR TEETH KICKED OUT?

Such a shame. Who would want to harm the loveable, docile walrus? Eskimos, that's who! They hate walrus's and hunt them all the time. Is it any wonder a rouge group of walrus finally broke away from the pack and moved south?

Think about it, you're a walrus, you're freezing your blubbery ass off sitting on a sheet of arctic ice. Men dressed in caribou pelts and yelling in a strange language are throwing harpoons at your wrinkled butt. What would you do? Pack up and move to Florida, that's what.

Surf, sand and plenty of sunshine, right? No more icebergs or sub zero temperatures, just crystal blue water and all the seaweed you can eat, right? Wrong!

Florida is crawling with hooligans. Bikers, gang members, restless teenagers, packs of roving grannies. All of them capable of kicking the tusks off a basking, unsuspecting walrus at any time. Face it, America can be a violent place. If you don't put up a fight in the face of adversity then there's going to be consequences. No creature can afford to just lounge out in the open and not expect some kind of confrontation from a redneck or a rebel. Sadly, all the walrus that made the adjerous journey from up north got their tusks kicked out and are now toothless and have been renamed *manatees.*

Although I must say, losing their teeth is a small price to pay in exchange for living in a tropical paradise like Florida.

DID YOU KNOW THAT McDonald's DOESN'T SERVE SCOTTISH FOOD?

You'd expect a place named McDonald's would specialize in authentic Scottish quizine, but there's no boiled potatoes on the McDonald's menu, no venison, wild boar or McHagus. You'd expect them to at least have Nessie burgers or Loch Ness nuggets or something of the like.

And by the way, how did Scotland become birthplace of the fast food revolution? It's not like Edinburgh or Glasgow are in the middle of the cheeseburger belt. Rare is the day you see a lonely bagpiper in kilt and bearskin hat silhouetted against the grey skies of Aberdeen, blowing on his pipes and sucking back a Big Mac in-between breaths. No, MacDonald's has about as much Scottish food as Burger King has royalty working the drive thru window. Let's all start sending complaint letters to the McDonalds corporation and demand that they start getting Scottish and start serving the disgustingly bland Scottish food we all know and love.

DID YOU KNOW THAT ELBOW MEAT IS THE EXACT SAME TEXTURE AS AN 86 YEAR OLD WOMAN'S NIPPLE?

Check it out! It's easy to do. Go find an old lady and ask her if she will help you conduct a little test. All she has to do is take her top and bra off for thirty seconds. If she agrees then the rest is simple. If at first she seems reluctant to comply I suggest baiting her with kindly offers of taking her to the mall or sitting with her as she reminisces of days gone by, or better yet, pretend you are an old flame come to visit from decades gone by.

Old ladies are forgetful and generally easy to fool in this way. Now, once your subject is prepared here's how to proceed. With your right hand, using your thumb and your pointing finger, gently tweak her ancient nipple, hold firmly and slowly roll the wrinkled nub back and forth, careful not to pinch too hard. You don't want the old lady to scream and have her smack you in the head with her purse.

Now, with your left hand, using the same fingers, grasp the wrinkled tuft of skin that covers either of your elbows. Once you have pinched a sufficient lump, simultaneously roll the old lady's nipple and your elbow meat back and forth in your fingers. If you close your eyes and don't look you will feel that they are exactly the same consistency in every way. It's really a foolproof test. If you're having trouble locating an old lady I suggest you contact a local seniors home. There are plenty of seniors around if one knows where to look for them. And always keep in mind that old ladies are people too and must be treated with the utmost dignity and respect. Always remember to clothe your subject when the experiment is done. Also, be sure to turn your senior in the direction of her place of residence before allowing her to wander aimlessly away away.

DID YOU KNOW THAT THERE WOULD BE INCALCULABLE FOOT INJURIES IF CARROTS GREW THE OTHER WAY?

We're all in agreement that carrots are a very, very pointy vegetable, probably the pointiest of all. So, that being said, imagine the ludicrous amount of personal injuries sustained if carrots grew the opposite way. Pointed side not into the ground but instead sticking up into the air like massive, rusted orange nails sticking out of an old two by four.

Imagine the number of feet that would have these beta-carotene spikes go right through their tender tootsies. Imagine the pain of a tapered, foot long, member of an important food group pushing through the sole of your foot, piercing flesh and bone only to pop up on the other side. People would be impaled and stuck to the ground where they stood. Farmers would have to harvest their crops while avoiding walking on a virtual carrot bed of nails. Who knows how many would lose their lives being crucified to the earths crust by these lethal vegetables. The rest of us would probably have to sport steel-toed boots and shoes anytime we dared to venture outside the paved safety of the city.

God forbid one should trip and fall in a carrot patch. There would be no way to move, no way to survive. So let's give thanks that *for now* carrots are subterranean. Enjoy it while you can because nature is forever changing and I'm certain it shant be long before man's most favored salad garnish becomes one of his most lethal, natural death traps.

DID YOU KNOW THAT PEOPLE WITH TWO DIFFERENT COLORED EYES ARE ACTUALLY HUSKIES?

As far as I know there is only one species of life that has two different colored eyes, meaning that one of its eyes could be brown and the other eye could be blue. This species, the majestic husky dog.

You've all seen them on the Discovery Channel, barking at roving polar bears or dragging an Eskimo sled across the barren Antarctic ice. But did you know there are also some "supposed" humans with two different colored eyes, singers David Bowie and Marylyn Manson, actress Kate Bosworth and Jane Seymour, actors Dan Aykroyd and Christopher Walken, even the late Alexander the Great had this condition.

Now, fancy scientists have labeled this symptom **hetero-chromia,** which to me is obviously a fancy Eskimo term meaning 'sturdy sled dog'. I think it's a bit shameful that we as a society try to shield this strange sub specie of humans hiding in our midst. It's time the 'Husky people' came out.

We all know the existence of werewolf's is the stuff of legend and folklore, but this collection of oddball husky people is real, we can see it, there's no hiding their eyes. If you don't believe me try throwing a slab of seal blubber at the feet of Christopher Walken and watch how furiously he snaps it in his jaws and consumes it with the vigor of a flesh hungry canine. Try cracking a whip behind Jane Seymour's back and watch her take flight like a horse out of the starting gate. Put the whole group together and watch David Bowie and Marilyn Manson fight to prove their pack leader superiority.

Watch all of them follow their natural instincts to take flight when strapped as a team to an Eskimo sled. Picture them charging across the ice fields and the tundra, persevering through a wintry blizzard, the steam from their breath in the cold air and their tongues hanging out and panting as they forge on across a desolate, cruel, and unforgiving frozen landscape. Yes, if you're ever at an important social function and happen to glimpse David Bowie urinating against a piano leg or a banister, now you'll know why. He's a husky.

DID YOU KNOW THAT SHAR-PEI DOGS CAN BE CURED WITH WRINKLE CREAM?

You've all seen Shar-Pei's, the "wrinkle dog". They're out at the dog park, being walked in the street, etc. Such a sad dog really. It's entire body just wave after wave of unsightly wrinkles. Rolls of flesh drooping over its ankles and continuing up it's legs, over its back and sides and finally culminating in a bumpy meat blanket that drapes right over its wrinkled up face. The poor beast can barley see due to the ripples of dog blubber wrinkled over its eyes. So, what's the cure? How does one take a Shar-Pei out of its misery, out of wrinkle hell? Well, thanks to the vanity of women all over the world, there is a remedy.

Common wrinkle cream was developed in the early 80's to help women fight the ravages of time, to soften their delicate features, remove wrinkles, and have us believe that a woman in her nineties is still a spry twenty six. Now, whether this actually worked or not I will leave up to you, but, the grand side effect is that Shar-Pei's everywhere now have a cure.

The process is simple. Generously cover your Shar-Pei in wrinkle cream three times daily for a span of six weeks. At about the four-week period you will see the wrinkles start to disappear and the true bloodline of your dog will begin to emerge. The anticipation is almost like working your way toward the prize at the bottom of a Cracker Jack box. Just what will your Shar-Pei turn out to be once it is cured? Is it a beagle under all those wrinkles? A rottweiler, a greyhound, a poodle? Whatever breed your Shar-Pei officially turns out to be, be sure to love it and take it for plenty of walks and destroy any old pictures you have of the unsightly "wrinkle years."

CHECKING IN WITH YOU!

Is this getting easier yet, or are you still in shock? Are you sitting there with this book in your lap, scratching your head and asking, "How did I not know this stuff? Where have I been? What have I been doing with my time?"

Hey, don't feel bad, you're not alone. Some of this stuff isn't easy. Some of it might even be stuff you weren't really sure you even wanted to know, but don't be like that. Remember, in life you can never know enough. The more you know the better off you'll be. So keep an open mind and be courageous. Let's keep flipping the pages because we have a lot more ground to cover. And speaking of *ground to cover*, did you know that if you were to cover the ground it would take your whole life and you'd still leave much of the planet exposed?

CHAPTER THREE

Thinking outside the cube

Now you're probably thinking, why did he write 'Thinking outside the *cube*' instead of *box*? Well, isn't a cube similar to a box? They're the same shape. You can put things in both, so why did I write cube? The answer is simple. To demonstrate how we sometimes think with blinders on our brains. That we are comfortable thinkers and don't want to strain too hard to attain new ideas, to absorb new concepts, or old ones as the case may be.

All around you are things you're not taking into account. Take a look at a wooden coffee table and what do you see? A slab of wood right? Wrong, I want you to look beyond the obvious. Picture the tree that was the source for the table, picture it as a seed, a sprout, a baby, a teenager, and then as a full grown, majestic pine, with thousands of needles and hundreds of pinecones. Picture it swaying gently with the summer breeze in a quiet forest. Ask yourself where the family of owls went that used to live in that tree. Ask yourself, did that tree want to be a place for people to lay their books and set their caffeine beverages? Or did that tree want to stand with its buddies and grow old quietly and with dignity?

Is a tree a coffee table? Is a cube a box? Are you a person or a human being? While you ponder these questions let's move on with your education.

DID YOU KNOW ANGEL HAIR PASTA TASTES BETTER IF SHAMPOOED?

Did you know that angels are making a killing by cutting their own hair and selling it to the worlds largest distributors of pasta? Although angels are angelic and live on a higher plain, you still shouldn't eat their hair without a thorough shampoo. Heaven is no doubt a beautiful place, but let's face it, with increased levels of commercial air traffic, residential, industrial, and recreational pollution, you have to figure an angel's hair is pretty greasy and grimy.

There's no way you can float in clouds all day and not absorb high levels of smog and exhaust fumes.

The next time you decide to sit down to a steaming bowl of angel hair pasta you might want to do this first. Cook pasta in pot of boiling water for three to four minutes, remove, and apply a generous amount of Head and Shoulders shampoo, or Pert Plus with revitalizing conditioners and aloe vera. Massage pasta thoroughly with fingers, scrubbing deep to the center of the pasta. Rinse under warm water, and repeat the process again. Now that your angel hair has a full-bodied shine, apply generous amounts of marinara, alfredo, or pesto sauce. Enjoy on your own or serve to a party of friends. Remember, any chef will tell you, clean food is good food. Enjoy.

DID YOU KNOW THAT SCARECROWS DON'T SCARE CROWS, THEY ATTRACT HOMELESS PEOPLE?

Crows are considered by naturalists and scientists alike to be one of the world's more intelligent birds. How long do you think it takes them to realize that the guy standing in the corn with the straw hat and the faded plaid shirt hasn't moved or changed his clothes in the last four days? My guess is that crows figure it out pretty quick. I think it's fair to say that scarecrows do not effectively scare crows the way say a laser gun or a land mine or a cannon might.

On the other hand, scarecrows have a much less desired effect, an effect that was unforeseen. Scarecrows inadvertently attract homeless people... that's right, homeless. Think about it, you're a homeless guy meandering up the road, tired, hungry, cold. There's nowhere to go, there's nowhere to eat, there's no respite in sight, until of course, you round that next bend and behold... a scarecrow!!

What could be more of an answered prayer to a homeless person? They see a scarecrow and it's essentially a new set of clothes free for the pickins, and what's better, the clothes are hanging on a stake in the middle of a field full of food. Rows of corn, lettuce, celery, beets, carrots, for as far as the eye can see. This is homeless persons utopia, a virtual Shangri-La for the needy. From aimlessly wandering in ripped and ragged clothes, to a sudden country boy look makeover. It's a win win. So, farmers be warned, even if you do happen to scare the odd crow with your scarecrow, be prepared for the humanitarian effort that comes with it. Caaaaaawwwww cccc caaaaaaaaawwwwwwwwwwwwww!!!

DID YOU KNOW THAT KFC IS JUST ONE LETTER AWAY FROM BEING ONE OF THE RUDEST WORDS IN THE ENGLISH LANGUAGE?

It used to be called Kentucky Fried Chicken, easy enough, right? Well, apparently not. The damn name is too long. Lazy Americans don't have the energy or stamina to verbalize such a long name, so, the geniuses at Kentucky Fried Chicken headquarters decided to make it easier on all of us and shorten the title to just it's initials **KFC**. Okay, fair enough. The quicker I finish talking the faster I can stuff a drumstick into my mouth. That's pretty good logic and some intelligent marketing. "Intelligent" that is until we realize how close to profanity we are.

Think about it, K F C, three of the prime letters of the most famous four-letter word in the universe. A word so appalling that I can't even spell it out in it's entirety lest I offend a young child, the elderly, a person of faith, or just a plain ol' chicken eating citizen of this great world of ours. So where does KFC get off tempting fate? Pushing the boundaries of civility by coming within a razors edge of the almighty 'F' word? If they graduated from the name Kentucky Fried Chicken, to the current KFC, then who's to say the name doesn't morph again and the worlds most beloved fried chicken just becomes know as F..ck!!

Can you imagine what a desensitized society we would become? "Mommy, I want to go to F..uk for dinner. I want F..ck fries and a Family F..ck Bucket please."

Yeah, I know, it's bad. We all better keep our eyes on this one. I mean what's next, a burger joint called Fuddruckers? Good luck to the dyslexic crowd pulling into to this place. Can you imagine the trouble they would have saying the name Fuddruckers?

"Mommy, I wan to go to Motherfu...... Well, you know the rest.

DID YOU KNOW THAT WOMEN WITH LONG FINGERNAILS LOVE TO HUNT SALMON?

Every spring the salmon come to spawn. They tirelessly swim up stream to lay their precious eggs and then die. Such determination, such will power, such an ultimate sacrifice. The salmon's journey is filled with obstacles and dangers unsurpassed anywhere in nature. The odds are completely stacked against these horny fish. Only the lucky ever make it to a suitable place where they can get it on.

Some of the elements in the salmon's path are raging rapids, waterfalls, parasites, disease, predatory birds and mammals, with one distinct predatory mammal topping the list. I know what you're all thinking, the grizzly bear! Well, you're wrong. There is one mammal of higher intelligence and of greater determination than even the mighty and fearless grizzly. It's women.

I'm talking housewives, receptionists, legal assistants, dentist, teachers, doctors, even supermodels. Yes, good old-fashioned *ladies.* In particular the ones who grow their fingernails over two or four inches long. Nails grown to such lengths can longer be considered cosmetic attractions. They must be labeled for what they really are, salmon fishing claws.

Women with such nails can be seen every spring crouched on the bustling shores of swollen, raging, rivers. Patiently they wait for unsuspecting salmon to swim by, and then *SWIIIISH,* with the speed, desperation and determination of a starving carnivore they swat the helpless fish from the icy waters and devour them on the pebbly shores.

Some women even lumber through the shallows and chase the sorry fish, wearing them down until they can no longer swim. And then, with the gusto of Freddy Kruger at a frat party, the long nailed women end the salmon's short-lived life with a lethal swipe from their killer claws.

Nature can be cruel at times and all we can do is sit back and observe.

DID YOU KNOW THAT 'IKEA' STANDS FOR Insufficient Knowledge Erecting Apparatus?

We've all followed the yellow arrows through IKEA. We've all been mesmerized by the perfect Swedish showrooms. "How grand that would look in my home!" we all think. So, we buy the Swedish bookshelf with the funny Swedish name, 'Blunka' shelves. Or the coffee table 'Slavi', or the wooden bed frame 'Solungderflunga'. How about just bookshelf, coffee table, bed? Do we have to have the stupid Swedish names? What, am I Swiss for crying out loud?? I just want to get my purchases home and have my house look like a Swedish showroom.

So, I get my stuff home, in a box by the way, and I start to pull out all the pieces. Slabs of wood, screws, hinges, more wood, some meatballs… it never ends. I just wanted a bookshelf, I didn't sign up to construct a six-foot Rubik's cube. I want a new bedroom not a jigsaw puzzle. And the instructions are no help. Stick screw A into hole B, slide slot C into slot H? Is this Kama Sutra or instructions to a book shelf? Okay, well I've come this far, I might as well put the damn thing together, I have seven hours to kill anyway, right? So, let me get my tool box and screwdriver…. And… wait… what??? I don't need traditional tools to put the three hundred pieces of wood together? What? I can do it all with this little four inch long cheap aluminum Allen wrench?? WOW! Nobody told me this was going to just keep getting better and better.

Okay, so now I have lumber spread throughout my living room, instructions that read like a Japanese play book, and a little Swedish screwdriver thingy that looks like a bent hockey stick, Great! This should be a no brainer. WRONG! Cut to ten hours later, the damn cabinet is finally assembled and you realize that you built it upside down, or backwards, or sideways, or the hinges are on the wrong side, or something has gone terribly wrong. In the end you just throw your mattress on the floor without the IKEA bed frame and sleep for hours and hours hoping you wake up and your Swedish, IKEA nightmare is over!

DID YOU KNOW THAT OCTOPUS AND SQUID EAT BALL POINT PENS AND PRINTER REFILL CARTRIGES?

Think about defending yourself. You're being attacked by a bunch of thugs in an alley behind a 24-hour Denny's, what do you do? Pick up a stick, an old pipe, a broken bottle? You try to defend yourself. You kick, you punch, you bite, pull hair, maybe even run. Fine, all acceptable defense responses, but would you ever spread your legs and squirt ink? Cause that's what octopus and squid do! They shoot office supplies at their enemies to shake em' off.

Now, have you ever seen a baby gazelle shooting paper clips at a pursuing cheetah? Have you ever witnessed a fleeing zebra drop a trail of thumb tacks in the path of a charging lion? No! Office supplies are not used in nature by most animals… except, the octopus and squid. So, where do they get this ink? It's not like it grows inside of them. What they do is sneak into office supply stores such as Staples or Office Depot during non-peak hours. They slink through the aisles searching for pens, Sharpies, markers, ink refill cartridges, anything to replenish their ammunition. It's scary. I don't want to be in Staples at two in the afternoon searching for a three-hole punch and then suddenly, there in aisle four I come face to face with a slithering sea serpent! Yikes. And how on earth did this bizarre tactic come to be in the first place? Obviously some marine biologist, ichthyology nerd was hanging his pimply face over the side of boat looking for shrimp or scallops or something exciting, and somehow a Bic slipped out of his pocket protector and fell into the mighty sea. It sunk to the ocean floor where it was scavenged by an octopi. It hungrily sucked the gooey ink from the pen and dined on it until it was gone. The next day the octopus was confronted by a large predatory fish. So startled was the octopi that he excreted himself. The toxic ink squirting into the hungry fish's face and consequently driving it away. All the other octopi and squid got wind of this miraculous event and ballpoint pen sucking was born. Funny how smart some animals can be. Now if we could only figure out why porcupines are such pricks!

DID YOU KNOW THAT CLAMARI RINGS ARE JUST DEEP FRIED BUTT HOLES?

Isn't it obvious? I mean look at the shape, the texture, the elasticity. Who are they trying to kid? You can't deep fry everything and get away with it. I know they deep fry wings, and fries, and shrimp, and some people do whole turkeys and Twinkies, but butt holes, c'mon man!! It's just not right. Somewhere in the world there is a town or village or city where the folks are walking funny cause they either sold their butt holes or had them forcefully taken in some kind of black market calamari ring operation. This is really cruel stuff.

Now, all that being said there is one small glitch in this parade of compassion for the butt-holess… Them calamari rings are delicious.

Most of us probably knew in the back of our minds what calamari rings really were. We all had inkling. And isn't it convenient that they "claim" that these yummy rings are actually slices of some deep-sea creature, the squid? A creature that none of us really have any access to. Notice that 60 Minutes has never followed up on the world of calamari? The squid claim is a lie. Nonetheless we hungrily pop them in our mouths, chew on their rubbery texture and with a satisfied cry proclaim, "I want some more of them deep fried butt holes!" In fact we even dip em' in sauce to further the culinary experience. So, enjoy your calamari rings, and if the saying holds true "you are what you eat" then that makes you one great big deep fried butt hole!

DID YOU KNOW THAT CAULIFLOWER IS JUST BROCCOLI THAT'S SEEN A GHOST?

If you do a comparison test and hold a head of cauliflower up to a head of broccoli you will see that there is very little difference, except for one. Cauliflower is completely white. Cauliflower is grown on haunted farms and is nothing more than broccoli that is traumatized by regular visits by ghosts.

Farmers raise fields of young broccoli and just before harvest they unleash spirits from the netherworld, lost souls in transition into the next plane. They allow these spirits to drift amongst the healthy green broccoli at will. The broccoli naturally have only one reaction. They look up and see the ghosts floating toward them and they lock up in fear, the same way we all would if approached by the undead. So horrified and traumatized are the young vegetables that they turn sheet white from the terror that courses through their leaves and fibers. It's unconsiable, to treat a respected member of a food group with such disregard. To raise a crop under such inhumane conditions is unforgivable. It's akin to the sufferable conditions in which we raise veal. I ask, is it farming or is it torture? And why, why do we do it? It is for one reason and one reason only. Something in the terror process changes the texture of broccoli. It must release some kind of hormone or adrenalin or tenderizer or something, because there is no denying that a cooked cauliflower is more subtle and tender than a cooked broccoli. And it is man's greed, man's insatiable appetite for anything that pleases his palate that allows this process to continue.

Until all the broccoli ghost farms of the world are shut down the haunting will continue. Young broccoli will be subjected to ghostly visits that turn their skin snowy white and in doing so satisfy the human need for scared broccoli. Let us all hope that this practice stops sooner rather than later and that we can stop using the souls of the dead to help us manipulate nature's design. As a final footnote may I suggest a creamy cheese sauce with your next cauliflower? Truly delicious.

CHAPTER FOUR

A little story

Let me tell you a little story. Once upon a time there were billions of people and they were all taught the same things. These billions of people were all given the same information throughout their lives and that pretty much seemed to be enough... for most of them. Birds fly, fish swim, two plus two is four, redheads are stupid.

We've all been fed the same data our whole lives. We all pretty much think the same and act the same and live the same. I know you want to protest and scream, "I'm an individual! I'm different", and sure, every now and then you break away from the norm and make some pottery or ride a horse or rock climb! "WOW! You did what? You climbed a rock? Holy smokes! So for a few moments you stood higher on the earth than the rest of us? Wooooow!!! You wanna go to the mall?"

I'm not trying to diminish your accomplishments, we all have them, we all do them, but when was the last time you sat down and really thought about something outside the context of what we've been programmed to know? Have you really pushed your brain to do anything new and astounding? That's the beauty in all this, you really can be an individual if you really think about it... make the effort, but let's face it, thinking different and deep is hard, it takes effort. Wouldn't you really rather eat Pringles and watch TV? And for those of you defiant ones who are thinking, "How dare he paint me with his broad brush of categorization. I'm not like all those other people. I'm not like everyone else". Of course not, we're all different in subtle ways, but our minds are so vast and deep and incredible I sometimes think we're scared to dive too deep into them.

For those that feel they have mined the depths of their grey matter I have to say that making a stock pick or having a weird dream or doing an impression of Christopher Walken doesn't count. Have you ever heard the story about a guy named George de Menstral? It's quite interesting. George was a Swiss Mountaineer who used to enjoy hiking in the hills with his dog. On one occasion the pair returned from a trek only to find themselves covered in burrs. The dog's hair was matted and Georges's pants were covered with the clingy plant seeds. Now, you or I would merely pluck a burr from wherever it was affixed, but not George, he put one under a microscope. It was then that he observed the tiny hooks that allowed the burr to cling to cloth and fur and fabric alike. Upon this discovery he decided he would create a two-sided fastener. One side would have tiny hooks as the burr did, and the other side would have tiny loops as found in fabric. He would call his invention VELCRO, a material all of us use during the span of our lifetime. So, what's the point you're asking? George was an inventor, "I'm just a schoolteacher or a security guard or a pilot." The point is George let his mind wander. Allowed his brain to think beyond what was the norm. By thinking deeper he found the potential in an annoying plant seed and turned it into something. I'm not saying you are going to be the next big inventor, but what I am saying is look around you. What do you see? What are you limiting yourself to see? What's really there in front of you? In your backyard, your living room, your life? What would happen if you sat down in a quiet room and set a timer for fifteen minutes? You sat there and said, "I'm gonna think of stuff I've never thought of before. I'm gonna go way outside the box and just be alone with my thoughts. I'm gonna think deep and hard and intense with no real subject in mind. I'm just going to let it come, push the gas peddle on my incredible mind and see what comes out?" Hmmmmmm what do you think would happen? Are you scared to try? Would you feel foolish? Feeling foolish is just being scared. Go ahead, try it. Sit in a quiet room and FORCE your brain to think. Fifteen minutes of sheer intensity, as if your mind is sprinting in a hundred yard dash, no letting up, no holding back, just pure brain rush for fifteen minutes.

I wonder what will flood your head? Will it give you a headache or will it change your life? Who knows? Don't be scared, give it a try, no one even has to know. Take a little time and sit with your brain awhile. Just the two of you. See what happens.

PART TWO

CHAPTER FIVE

ARE YOU FEELING GROOVY?

Okay, are you feeling groovy yet? I hope so. Why not? It's always fun to learn new things. Remember the first time you learned how to read, ride a bike, or that girls had no wieners? Those were big moments in your lives, they were areas of your existence that didn't exist and then suddenly, they did! How weird is that? Not knowing how to read, to reading. Not riding a bike, to riding. And I'll leave the learning about no wiener experience up to you. The thing is, new thoughts and ideas are groovy. They make us who we are. So lets keep on motoring and feed the flames of knowledge. This is your time to expand, grow, open your mind and let the goodies flow in. You're like a reverse piñata.

DID YOU KNOW THAT DOGS DON'T KNOW HOW TO OPEN CHRISTMAS PRESENTS?

Every Christmas people put wrapped presents under the Christmas tree for their pet dogs. They even write their dogs name on the package to ensure that the dog doesn't accidentally open the wrong gift. "To Scrappy, Love Mommy." I don't know if you know this or not but dogs A: Don't read, and B: cant tear off gift wrapping. They don't even have hands. If left to its own devices a dog would sooner urinate under the tree and water his own gifts before having a clue as to opening them.

Dogs don't understand boxes with red and green wrapping with pictures of an old guy with a white beard. They don't appreciate bows and ribbons, all dogs' want is meat. When you ask your dog on Christmas morning "where's your present boy? Go get your present!" he has no idea what you're talking about. He has no idea that Jesus, the son of the creator is having a birthday. You rarely see dogs at church. So, when you drag that box from under the tree and put it at your dog's feet and he just looks up at you with a facial expression that says, " What is this? I can't eat this." Don't be disappointed. Although you made the effort to include Rover in the festivities, he's clueless.

Dog's don't unwrap Christmas presents, they don't weld, they can't fly helicopters. Treat your dog like a dog. Take him to the park and let him sniff some ass and eat a squirrel. You do that and believe me, that dog is having Christmas everyday.

DID YOU KNOW THAT YOUR ZODIAC SIGN IS ON MORGAN FREEMAN'S FACE?

What a great actor Morgan Freeman is. So subtle yet, so powerful. He commands the screen and his soft purposeful voice draws us in every time. Surely one of America's finest. But there is another subtlety to Mister Freeman that most of you, if not all of you overlook. It's the many speckles that dot Mr. Freeman's face. They look like freckles but at the same time appear to be something else. A skin disorder perhaps, some kind of blemish, rash, pimples? I have never had the pleasure of caressing Mr. Freeman's face, so one cannot be too sure. But what is sure is that there are many of them. Whatever they are, they are aplenty! Some might say like the multitude of stars that hang so beautifully in the night sky. Like the blanket of star clusters that line the milky way. And in keeping with that theme, there is something else. If you watch Mr. Freeman's face in a close up during a movie, or locate an image of his face in a magazine or on the Internet, you will see that in his vast array of speckles lies a map of our solar system. It is in this map of the heavens that you can spot such familiar star formations as the big dipper, Orion's belt, the North Star, and many others. To my delight, and to yours I would assume, one can also identify the stars that compose the twelve known signs of the zodiac. Yes. There on his left cheek sits Virgo, Cancer and Leo. To the right of his nose and spanning toward his temple are spread Capricorn, Sagittarius, and of course my favorite, Scorpio. Yes, my birth sign right there on an 'A' list celebrity's face, an Oscar winner no less.

It warms me to see Scorpios stinger curled right up under a prominent Hollywood figureheads lower left eye. Can you spot your sign? Does it become animated, move and come to life when Mr. Freeman laughs or frowns.

Truly this man is able to make the stars dance in the sky with his every facial expression. I could stare into that mans face forever. And sometimes, if you're lucky and Mr. Freeman is shooting an outdoor scene, you might by chance see a fly buzz past his face, and in that moment one can only imagine one is seeing a rare glimpse of one of our proud space shuttles streaking across orbit. We picture the brave astronaut crew floating inside as they explore the vast frontiers of space for the future of mankind. Yes, Morgan Freeman, what an actor, what a human being, what a space face!

DID YOU KNOW THAT GAY PEOPLE CANT SAY "DAMN STRAIGHT?"

Over the decades scientist, politicians, religious groups, and moral leaders have argued about the source of homosexuality. Some believe it to be hereditary others believe it is acquired, some believe people are born with it and still others believe it is a lifestyle that is "chosen." Many often wonder how you can truly determine if one is gay. Some people struggle with their own sexual preferences and orientation. Some wonder "Am I gay or am I not? What are these feelings I'm experiencing? Why does Bob look so delicious in those light brown, corduroy jeans?" Many of us have a family member or friend that we suspect may be gay but has never opened up to us about it. In fact, most of us have asked ourselves at least one point in our lives "could I be gay?" It's only natural to wonder. It's the same way we wonder about anything in our lives, it's merely a question. "Will I ever get married? Have kids? Live in Finland?" It is human to question ourselves. The "gay" question is scary because the answer may come as unexpected. The answer may mean a drastic change in your lifestyle, your social circles, your clothing, your hair, your outlook. Whether the outcome is good or bad is entirely up to you. Nobody knows your beliefs or comfort level better than you. So, how do we figure out who's truly who?

This is a mixed up society we live in. Most of the time we cant determine who is what anymore, so here's the answer. It's simple. Gay people cannot speak a simple phrase that we all know and use in our everyday language, gay people can not say the words,"*DAMN STRAIGHT!!*" It just can't be done.

We all know the phrase, you hear it on the farm, at the office, at football games, "Man, that Brady can really throw a football!" to which an associate replies " Damn straight!" Or another example, picture a young freckled faced boy talking to his older cowboy cousin on the sidelines at a rodeo. "You really gonna go in that ring and ride that bull cousin Eddy?" To which Eddy calmly replies, "Damn straight!" And then he spits on the ground and sniffles. But gay people, no way. They can't get through this phrase if they try. For example, a football player is getting his hair quaffed at a Beverly Hills salon and says, " Damn Pasqual, you are really good with that hair dryer." To which Pasqual attempts, "Damn st... stra.. st.. st.. st.. str...aaaaaaaaaahhhhhhh." And BANG, right there you know he's gay. He can't complete the phrase. So there it is people. You can put away the psychology tests and the bible and the 60 minutes investigations. If you want to know who's straight and who's not, go to the nearest mirror and see if you can say the phrase *"DAMN STRAIGHT!"*

DID YOU KNOW THAT GIRAFFES ARE JUST LEOPARDS THAT GOT THEIR HEADS STUCK IN AN ELEVATOR DOOR?

Leopards and giraffes are the same animal. I know it's hard to believe but it's true, I mean just look at their spots. It's undeniable. Leopards are one of the most cunning and elusive big cats that we see in the wild. It's safe to assume that they are such masters of stealth and disguise that they are no doubt living amongst us. In our neighborhoods, our parks, our garages, and yes I'm positive they lurk in the hallways and boardrooms of office buildings and department stores.

This theory can be proved by simply looking closely at the common giraffe and comparing it to the leopard. Same markings, same density of fur, living in the same regions in Africa as the leopard. Mere coincidence? I think not.

Let's go back to what I said about leopards being amongst us, in our man made structures.

Within most of our multi level architectural creations there exits elevators. A common device used to transport us humans from one floor to the next. A simple piece of apparatus to operate for us humans, but throw one of Africa's top predators in an elevator and it is almost rendered useless. Leopards do not posses the skills to successfully negotiate a simple elevator. As a result they often und up trapped in elevator doors as they close. As the mighty cats step cautiously from elevators they are momentarily confused and perplexed by the 'dinging' sounds, and the humming of motors and the slick sound of sliding metal doors. This combined commotion freezes the mighty hunter in its tracks, and sadly, very often right in the elevator door, doorframe. Consequentially, the doors slide shut and trap the spotted killer's like a monkey in quicksand.

Powerless, the leopard's helpless cries and howls can be heard reverberating through the buildings, and as you know, we humans hate nothing more than an animal in distress. So, regardless of the dangers to us, the humans assemble to try and free the unfortunate leopards. Everyone helps in the cause, compassionate office workers, janitors, security guards, mailroom clerks, and even senior management, all rally together to free the trapped beasts.

It is here, during the rescue operation that a most incredible transformation takes place. Humans cautiously approach the agitated mammal and delicately grab its flailing paws, it's neck, its face. In unison they pull, straining with all their might. It's animal against machine, one of natures most horrible and played out themes. It's a game that nature rarely wins.

With nothing but good intentions the humans give it their all, but rarely does a determined elevator door ever give up its catch. The result is as follows.

Slowly but surely the spotted cat begins to stretch. First its face, going from blunt and round to elongated and softer in appearance. Its snout and lips pulled to triple the length. Next is naturally the neck. As a tug of war plays out with the elevator the helpless cat's vertebrae and skin are pulled to well over nine feet. The only upside to this is that it allows other patrons of the building to move in and get a hold of the subject and help with the pulling. With this added muscle power it is common for the cat's upper body to be pulled free from the door. But not wanting to give up the fight, the elevator quickly snaps shut on the back legs of its prey. Now the battle intensifies. Two dozen or more humans are pulling the leopard by its head, neck, and front arms. As the back legs remain anchored in the elevator doors they also begin to stretch. The beautiful cat has become like an elastic band. Its front and back legs now pulled to lengths of over seven or eight feet.

Finally, as the struggle comes to an end, the cat is freed, a word I use loosely. Freed yes, but will forever bare the scars of its unfortunate encounter. It went into the elevator as a cat and came out as a giraffe. From a graceful predator with the ability to move silently and effortlessly through plains and jungles, to a tall, lanky, awkward horse looking creature that couldn't hide if it tried.

Although it is tragic the way giraffes are made, the upside is we are treated to two beautiful animals that help fill our amazing and varied ecosystem.

DID YOU KNOW DRESSING YOURSELF AS A PINATA AT HALLOWEEN WILL GET YOU BEATEN TO DEATH?

There are a million and one things you can dress up as for Halloween and not endanger your life. So play it safe and *do not* dress up in a piñata costume. Go out trick or treating as Spiderman, the Hulk, a witch or a pirate. Dressing up as a multi colored burro with big excited eyes, erect ears and a toothy grin will get you pretty near beaten to death. You might as well dress as Rodney King and trick or treat at the door of a local police station. People like to hit piñata's, they like to hit them hard, with sticks and bats, split em' open until the insides drop out. Is that what you want? To have the Three Musketeers bars beaten out of you on Halloween night? As if this warning weren't enough, there is an amendment… do not go trick or treating as a piñata in a Latino neighborhood. Spanish people are nuts for piñata's, they love them. They will chase you through the streets swinging any kind of object they can find, bat's, sticks, canes, shopping carts, you don't stand a chance. An unruly mob will form and you will be pursued through the streets and alleys with all the vim and vigor of a merry ol' English foxhunt. There will be nowhere to run, nowhere to hide. Your rainbow bright markings will stand out even on the darkest of chilly autumn nights. And should you think to form an alliance with a group of nearby kids dressed as trolls, ghosts, zombies, Superman's, and kitty cats, you will quickly learn what a mistake that is, for they will turn on you faster than the Lord of the Flies boys turned on poor chubby, little Piggy. In the end they hunted him down and ran him off a steep cliff. As a piñata marked for a beating you stand a good chance of being run off a highway overpass should you decide to flee from the kids. So, take my advice, go buy yourself an Iron Man or ladybug costume, anything but a piñata. In doing so you will be assured of many a fabulous 'Snicker's Mini Bite' filled Halloweens to come.

CHAPTER SIX

DON'T LECTURE ME ZUCCINI ASS!!

I wouldn't dream of lecturing you. That's not what this book is. Think of this book as a shwelp fleshelp book. Huh? That's right, what I just said has no meaning. It's just a bunch of random letters I threw together. They're not even words. So "why'd I do it?", you ask. And I say, "why the heck not?"

Every word you're reading right now is just a bunch of random letters that we decided if put together in the right sequence would form a word that if read we would associate with a person place or thing, or if heard would register meaning from the sound the assembly of letters makes when vocalized. So who's to say I just can't make up a word or two? Why not? It's not like there's no room for them. It's not like if there are too many words we will hit a word quota. So, as another blatant example of how we are all tuned in only on a few channels, I offer unto you the power of change. It may not seem practical to create words but someone has to do it. Five years from now there will be new words that didn't exist. They will be born the same way galaxy's are. Think of all the new words in the last decade, blog, gamer, Twitter, crayneeol, ok, again, the last one I made up. But why not? The key here is to be a forward thinker. Try to envision what isn't yet there. Try to imagine or create that which is meant to be. Someone has to do it. Why are you waiting for everyone else? Try to look at things from your rich, creative mind. Share an idea with someone that leaves them scratching their head. It'll be fun for you. C'mon, just give it a shot zucchini ass.

DID YOU KNOW THAT SEEING EYE DOGS ONLY CHASE CARS AROUND BLIND CORNERS?

Canines love a good car chase. I'm not sure what it is about cars that they despise so much, but somehow they feel the need to tear after them and snap veraciously at their rubbery wheels. To what end, remains a mystery. What on earth would they do with a car if they actually caught it? Gnaw through the metal? Urinate on the engine?

Drive to the coast for a sunset? It's not clear. What is clear is that most dogs are undisciplined and can be unruly and spontaneous. Bolting from their leashes, snapping and barking without provocation. Striking fear into the hearts of those of us unexpecting of these actions. But there is one rare dog that lives a very disciplined life, who never seems to stray from his routine. This breed is a calm, kind, and compassionate dog, I'm referring to the magnificent 'seeing eye dog'.

What an incredible animal. It comes in many different forms, lab, retriever, sheppard, collie, and yes, even mutts. Ever the patient guardian, this friend to man dedicates its life to aiding the sightless. Carefully, day in and day out guiding blind people through the perils and obstacles of every day, modern living. Rarely do we see these specialists at play. Seeing eye dogs have forfeited their normal dog life for that of a caregiver. These dogs navigate street crossings over catching Frisbee's and barking at people in uniform.

So how do these dogs have their recreational needs fulfilled? What do they do for fun?

The answer lies at any blind corner on any typical road that may exist in your city or town. The clever Seeing Eye dog lies in wait for any unsuspecting vehicle to careen around the corner. Being the blind specialists that they are the Seeing Eye dog makes its move and chases cars around these precarious bends in the road. So, next time you take a blind corner be warned, a very special animal is waiting... waiting to bite a hole in your rear tire and chase you until it runs out of breath and your car fades out of sight over the horizon.

DID YOU KNOW THAT THE WORD 'DYSLEXIC' IS THE PRIMARY CUASE FOR DYSLEXIA WORLDWIDE?

Are you kidding me?? Look at this damn word! 'Dyslexic', its got an 'X' and a 'Y' and an 'S' and a 'C'! How can all those crazy letters all be in one word? Just looking at the damn word gets my mind all mixed up.

I know that right now I am in the early throws of dyslexia, and the reason is the word dyslexia. I can't think straight. I can't look at other words now without my mind putting things all backwards and out of order. What the hell have you done to me dyslexia? You should not be a word. You should not be spelled the way you are and you should not be allowed to cause the very affliction that you are titled.

That's like Lou Gerrig getting Lou Gerrig's disease. It's unthinkable and unfair. And thas't all I hvea to sya!

DID YOU KNOW THAT ONION RINGS CAN BE USED TO MEASURE THE SIZE OF A MAN'S PRIVATES?

As unorthodox as it may sound it is very true. When it comes to a man measuring the size of his penis a tape measure can be very dangerous. It is sharp edged, metal, cold, and could potentially cause an uncomfortable laceration on your Twinkie stick. So, what is a safe alternative? How does a man determine the size of his piggy in a blanket without doing bodily harm to oneself? Amazingly the answer comes from the scrumptious world of fast food. Yes, I am speaking of delicious, golden, onion rings. They are the perfect size to comfortably slip over your bongo pole. They can easily accommodate any and all widths and lengths.

The average order of onion rings usually has up to fifteen or more. If you feel certain that your corncob is extra large, then by all means place a back up order as you roll through the drive thru. Also, Onion rings are extremely soft, pliable, and emit a pleasant odor. Finally, a fun and safe way to document the size of our mozzarella sticks. It's so easy and surprisingly accurate. Here's all one needs to do to get accurate measurement results.

Pick up the onion rings at your favorite fast food establishment; drive to a private place, your home, a public restroom etc. (Do not perform this function while seated in your car, it could result in a car accident or an arrest for public exposure.) Once seated in a suitable and comfortable surrounding, proceed to pull down your pants and allow you muskrat to be fully exposed. You may conduct the test in either a flaccid or erect state, this will all depend on your curiosity levels. Whichever you choose the process is as follows.

Carefully remove onion rings from the fast food bag and slowly begin stacking them, one on top of the other, over your pink microphone.

Continue to stack the delicious rings until finally the tip, or head, of your magic shillale can no longer be seen. At this point take an accurate count of how many golden onion rings it required to encase your spring roll. Once the data has been verified you are now free to discard the onion rings. It is not recommended they be consumed at this point. Also, always allow the onion rings to cool off before dropping them on your hairless rat. The last thing you want is testicle burn. Finally, now that you know how you "stack up", share with your friends. Don't be afraid to compare. Find out who can stack the most rings. Could you be the Lord of the Rings amongst your circle of friends?

See you at the Drive Thru!

DID YOU KNOW BI-POLAR IS NOT A SPECIES OF BIG, WHITE, BEAR, THAT SWINGS BOTH WAYS?

Bi-polar condition is a serious mental disorder that generally seems to affect the human race. It has been determined that a bi-polar person can have effects ranging from severe depression to extreme mood swings and unpredictable behavior. Caused by chemical imbalances and deficiencies in the brain, this troubling condition can be tough to manage for both the afflicted and those close to them.

Many people, including Eskimos have believed that bi-polar was in reference to the world's largest carnivore, the majestic polar bear. Many have been under the illusion that polar bears, despite their rugged reputation, may actually be involved in bi-sexual activity. This is an argument that has no foundation, no proof, or hard data to back it up. It is purely hearsay. No naturalist, biologist, zookeeper, or scientist has ever gone on record pronouncing that they have witnessed a male polar bear engaging in lude and erotic behavior with both a female and another male of its same species. Most of the professionals in the field still feel that polar bears are more interested in seal blubber than they are in experimenting sexually in a very cold and undeserving locale.

It is agreed worldwide that polar bears are much too rugged and tough to show any keen interest in an alternative lifestyle. Says noted biologist, Samuel Goldenmyer, from the National Institute of Sexual Bear studies, "Polar bears love walrus meat." Perhaps it is our own interpretation of how we want animals to be that causes bi-polar confusion. Perhaps we as a society are leaning on nature too hard with our own ideas of what's erotic and what's not. We must stop projecting our sexual agenda onto other living creatures that don't understand perverse human desire."

I hope this helps clear up any confusion about bi-polar disorder.

DID YOU KNOW THAT MAKING CANDLES FROM EARWAX WILL MAKE YOUR HOUSE SMELL LIKE THE INSIDE OF YOUR HEAD?

For whatever reason, God created us with wax in our ears. I'm not sure why. Some scientific explanations are, it was meant to repel insects and keep bugs from crawling in our heads, or an orchestras violinists or cellists use it in emergencies as a replacement for rosin. Whatever the answer may be there is one thing we most certainly should not use earwax for, and that is making candles.

God knows there's enough blueberry, cinnamon, and cranberry scented candles out there. Does it make any sense to add one that smells like the inside of our heads? Yes, it's true. If you were to save years worth of orangey, yellowy earwax and eventually shape it into a candle and then burn it, the result can fairly easily be predicted. Your house will reek with the scent of the inside of your head. Earwax is manufactured in your skull, it is churned or distilled or incubated in the inner part of your eardrums. Again, its function is not clearly known. What is known is that making your home smell of your inner head is both inappropriate and possibly unhygienic. What if someone were to breath in microscopic particles of your mind as the particles wafted innocently through the air in your nicely furnished living room?

What if those particles were smarter or dumber than the person who ingested them? Would *they* in turn get smarter or dumber? People might misinterpret the scent of your head and draw the grisly conclusion hat you are a cannibal and are stewing human flesh on the stove. People in general do not enjoy the scent of burning human innards. Any good crematorium custodian can attest to that.

If people really want to smell the inside of your head then they can damn well approach the side of you and stick their noses in your ear and take a long, deep, sniff. There is no need to flaunt the scent of the innards of your head.

Stick to candles from the Pottery Barn or Pier 1 and leave your wax in your head.

DID YOU KNOW THAT GREAT BLUE HERONS AND GREAT WHITE SHARKS AREN'T REALLY THAT GREAT?

How did an elegant marsh bird and the most feared creature on planet earth get the moniker 'great' put before their names?? 'Great' is a pretty big word to be throwing around isn't it? I mean Martin Luther King was great, freshly baked chocolate chip cookies are great, the movie Blade Runner was great, but a blue heron? What is so 'great' about a gangly bird that stands on one leg and hunts frogs and minnows all day? If that's all I have to do to achieve greatness then get me some hip waders, some sun block and a harpoon. Please, throw me in the bulrushes and let the greatness begin. Anyone for frog's legs??

And the 'great' white shark? Give me a break. If hunting seals, biting surfers in half and terrorizing Robert Shaw, Roy Schider, and Richard Dreyfuss, constitutes greatness then get me some metal braces, some flippers, and a map to the stars homes. I can't wait to be great! We have to be careful about special words such as 'great'. They can't be overused or misused or they lose their impact. Awarding fish and birds greatness without any apparent entitlement to such a high honor is a disservice to both our language and our society.

In the future lets just think of the blue heron and the white shark as just that. If one day I see either of the species splitting an atom, developing an alternative fuel to oil, or resolving starvation in the third world countries, then I might think of them as great. Until that day let me rename you the 'so, so' blue heron and the 'not bad' white shark.

DID YOU KNOW THAT CAJUN PEOPLE DON'T KNOW HOW TO SPEAK?

And I think we all agree that's all that pretty much needs to be said about that.

CHAPTER SEVEN

BLEEBLEE BLAH!

Well, congratulations. You've made it this far through all my bleee bllee blahblah blee. Which tells me you must be enjoying yourself or you would have put my ramblings down a long time ago. This is good. This is an indication to me that you are being a sponge and absorbing, taking in the new factoids that I am fertilizing your mind with. I'm glad.

It warms me inside to see that you have the courage to open up and if not accept new ideas at least give them a fair listen. It has been my experience in life to find lasting memories and joy in the few moments that didn't fit into the daily pattern of life. Little things and big things that didn't make sense in a world and a life style that becomes very familiar.

I can never forget a time in my early twenties when I was working in northern Canada as a forest ranger of all things. One of my duties was to lead a crew on a seven-day canoe trip through some of the most remote wilderness the country had to offer. On day three or four we were snaking our way through a narrow marsh, the width of the river probably no more than four or five feet across. We glided through the beautiful swamp grass and took endless turn after turn. This was some of the most serene wilderness I had ever seen. I wondered if any other humans had ever even been here before. Well, the answer soon came as I rounded the next bend in the meandering waterway. Something on my left side caught my eye, something totally out of place. It wasn't a tree or a rock or any kind of natural oddity, it was a sign. Yes, out here in the middle of nowhere, in the middle of God's great wilderness somebody had made a little sign, put it on a post and hammered it into the mud and the swamp grass. The sign read 'LARRY'S FISH AND CHIPS – ONE MILE', with an arrow pointing down the river.

I couldn't believe my eyes. To me it was one of the funniest things I had ever seen. It was so random and so out of place. I knew there was nothing around us for hundreds of miles, let alone a fish and chip shop in the middle of this rugged, vast, wilderness. I will never know who put that sign there but to this day I thank them. Things being where they "supposedly" aren't supposed to be, is a good thing. It reminds us to keep an open mind and to imagine.

Now…. go take an egg out of your fridge and sit on it for ten minutes and see what happens. Am I joking? Maybe, maybe not. I'll leave it up to you to decide. In the meantime let's start spreading your brain a bit more and continue canoeing through your mind.

DID YOU KNOW THAT PEOPLE WITH HAIRY MOLES ARE REALLY CATFISH?

Unsightly as facial moles may be they play an important role in our society. They help us to decipher who in fact is a catfish and who in fact is human. If you look closely you will notice that most facial moles have a hair or two growing out of them. They protrude from the brownish lumps like the distinguishable whiskers of the common catfish. It's fair to say that not all humans are created the same and at times genetic deficiencies or physical imperfections do sneak through.

In the case of the hairy mole it is beyond obvious that the people playing host to the mounds of brown fall into the 'are not human' category. Although many "Catfish people" attempt to hide their lineage by trimming or cropping their whiskers, it is to no avail. Inevitably they always grow back, and why? Because that is natures design. A cat is not a dog and a pelican is not a turtle. It is therefore easy to declare that catfish cannot be people. Marylyn Monroe, Cindy Crawford, Erron Neville, all catfish. If you visit their homes I guarantee you that they all have swimming pools in their yards. Coincidence? I think not. Where there's catfish there's water. You can hide your catfishness by starring in a movie or strutting down a catwalk or singing on the Tonight Show, but sooner or later, the fish always has to return to the sea.

I'm not prejudiced against the catfish people I just wish they would come out. Stop trying to masquerade who they are. Take a dip in a fountain. Shower yourself with mineral water at a fine restaurant, swallow a couple of fishing lures at a sporting goods shop. What I'm saying is… just be you. Catfish are people too! (sort of)

DID YOU KNOW THAT GETTING NAKED AND RUNNING BACKWARDS THROUGH CORN COULD DAMAGE YOUR COLON?

We've all done stupid things in our lives, you know, left the stove on, locked our keys in the car, forgot to set the alarm clock. We all feel stupid when we do these things, but they pass and we usually learn from the mistake. But one of the dumbest things you could ever do is get completely butt ass naked and run full speed, backwards through a cornfield.

Whatever you do, take it off your 'to-do list' right now! It would be just a matter of time until a jutting cob found a home right in your colon. This could prove to be a very painful injury, or in some cases a completely erotic experience. It all depends on how you look at it. In any case try to avoid attempting this exercise. Find a treadmill or go walk a dog or something. Corn on the cob is a summer time treat not a suppository. Be smart and keep your clothes on. Run forwards and good luck getting where you want to go.

DID YOU KNOW THAT ASSASIAN, LEE HARVEY OSWALD, WAS TRYING TO SHOOT A KFC?

You have to be extremely bitter and angry to want to try and shoot one of America's most beloved presidents. But on a sunny day in November, 1963, a shot rang out in Dallas Texas that changed history forever. A lone gunman, Lee Harvey Oswald fired his rifle into the streets and took the life of the late, great, JFK.

Oswald always proclaimed his innocence and denied that he was responsible. But, if he truly was guilty then we would all have to believe that a man was so filled with hate that he took the life of the worlds most powerful leader. But what if we don't believe? There's no denying that dozens of theories abound regarding the circumstances of the assassination. No one *really* seems to know exactly what happened on that grim day. So I have one more possibility to offer up.

What if the whole thing was a mistake? What if Lee Harvey was a vegetarian? What if he hated meat and the people that eat it? What if he hated establishments that sold meat products to consumers? Let's say chicken for example. And lastly, lets say Lee Harvey Oswald was not a good speller.

With all these fragments of a puzzle now before us, let's begin to put them together and reconstruct the sad events that unfolded that day. Let's try to set the record straight and if needs be, rewrite the pages of history.

So, here's Lee Harvey Oswald, a loner, a bad speller, and a hater of commercial meat products. He catches wind of a big event in Dallas, JFK is coming. In Lee's mind he jumbles the letters and he hears that "KFC is coming". Now the vegetarian's blood starts to boil. He doesn't want fast food chicken in his town. Angered and pumped up on cauliflower juice, he grabs a rifle and climbs the stairs to his familiar post in the book depository. A place where he often came to read in secret and work on his flawed ability to spell.

As JFK's motorcade moves down the street Lee Harvey leans out the window thinking the hoopla is for the opening of a new KFC. Blind with outrage Oswald opens fire at a building across the street that he thinks looks like a KFC. His shots miss and accidentally strike the president. Lee Harvey Oswald accidentally shoots JFK while trying to shoot a KFC. And the rest my friends, as they say, is history.

DID YOU KNOW THAT WEB DESIGNERS WILL EAT YOU?

Be very wary of dating a web designer. There is a very strong possibility you will never be seen again. Picture this, you meet a cute girl or guy. There's a mutual attraction so you agree to go on a casual date, a simple coffee or a quiet dinner, whatever. You get settled in, you start talking to each other, have a glass of wine, it all seems to be going great. So, naturally during the course of your encounter you ask them what they do for a living. The answer seems innocent enough, "I'm a web designer."

Hey, in this technilogical age it makes sense right? No problemo! As the hour grows late he or she invites you back for a nightcap or a game of Risk or something. Things have gone relatively well so you agree to the proposition and off you go.

Cut to a small, cozy apartment. You start to kiss and fondle and eventually the action takes you into the bedroom. It's not long before the clothes come off and you ready yourself for some adrenalin filled monkey business. But as you lay there naked on your back in anticipation of your new lover, you notice something. Is it the dim lighting? Is it the angle she is standing at? You notice something odd as she disrobes. Something seems out of the ordinary. As she stands naked at the end of the bed you swear you can see some added appendages. Are your eyes playing tricks on you? What are those things? Does she have an extra arm or two?

As your mind reels and you try to shake off the extra glass of wine you consumed, you notice the look on her face has changed. Her lustful, playfulness has been replaced by a look of what can only be described as a maniacal hunger. As you try to determine how and why the mood suddenly feels different and strange it is already too late. The appendages you thought you saw now come into full view. Eight fuzzy legs unfolding like leathery tent poles. Your mind reels, unable to comprehend the abnormal abboration that is morphing before your terror filled eyes.

Now the legs are exposed and they immediately go to work, carrying your once attractive date up the wall and on to the ceiling. And now she hangs overhead looking at you pinned to the bed, paralyzed with fear, unable to swallow at the very sight of the achroid legs. This is madness. A beautiful, free spirited rendezvous has now evolved into kiss of the spider woman. And before you can stammer, "What the hell is going on?" it hit's you, "Web designer! She's a godamn web designer.

But before you can protest it's already too late, for now feathery strands of web drift down over your helpless body, encasing you in a silky tomb from which you shall never escape. Soon you are immobile and at the web designers mercy as she effortlessly hauls you toward the ceiling and into her inescapable grasp. And as her long, spidery arms embrace you and her fork like mandibles puncture your tender neck, you realize one last thing.

As your blood drains from your body and feeds her pulsing, heaving abdomen, you make a final mental note to... "Never date a web designer."

DID YOU KNOW THAT COUNT CHOCULA IS THE ONLY VAMPIRE IN THE WORLD WITH BUCK TEETH?

Whether you believe in vampires or not, one thing is pretty much unanimous, all vampires have fangs. Fangs are indeed their trademark. Long, pointed, dagger like canine teeth. Just to envision them is enough to make ones blood turn cold.

For centuries we have been terrified by the very mention of a vampire. Our deepest fear is to fall victim to their seductive and mesmerizing presence. To let our guard down and expose the soft, tender skin that covers our necks. To feel the painful, yet pleasurable puncture of the vampires bloodthirsty mouth on our throats.

Fear as we might, there is one citizen of this murky underworld of living dead who we perhaps need not fear. One vampire who I dare say may be an outcast or a mutant or even some kind of hillbilly. I'm talking of course about the surprisingly well know creature of the night know as Count Chocula. A vampire indeed, but at the same time somewhat of an oddity.

At first glance he seems to be a traditional vampire, you know, the cape, the big hair, high eyebrows, long fingernails. But when one examines the good Count's mouth there awaits a startling anomaly. Unlike all other vampires with their pointed fangs, Chocula is the one and only vampire with abnormally large buckteeth. In fact he is the only vampire that has elongated incisor teeth instead of the traditional canines. The result is a poor mans vampire that looks neither frightening nor intimidating. In fact he's almost downright laughable. I can only imagine the extent of the damage he could do to ones throat. Maybe leave some teeth marks? Maybe leave a bruise? I doubt very much that Count Chocula's chompers could ever penetrate the skin. And what makes matters even more laughable is that this vampire appears to have more of a taste for chocolate and cocoa over the warm, salty, delicacy of human blood? What the hell is wrong with this guy? I don't want to wake up on a moonlit night to see a vampire at my window staring in at the unfinished glass of Swiss Miss instant cocoa on my night table. That could almost be taken as insulting. Ridiculous, a chocolate loving vampire with a sweet tooth. What's next, Frankenstein with strawberries painted on his fingernails?? Sheeeeesh.

DID YOU KNOW THAT IF WE ABOLISHED ALL SILENT LETTERS WE COULD CREATE NEW WORDS?

There are a lot of silent letters out there, letters that don't really need to be there. There's a silent 'h' in school and ghost. A silent 'c' in scissors. Almond has a silent 'l', as does salmon. Anybody got a bad case of asthma? Cause I got a bad case of an extra 'th' in that word.

What about Chanukah? How do I celebrate a religious holiday whose letters don't match the sound? How about Hunnaka, anyone? Hello! I mean whom do we go to about this blatant waste or overuse of letters? We can't go to Oprah cuz she has a silent 'h' at the end of her name so she won't be on our side. What we need to do is take all these silent letters and put them together in one new word so they don't have to be out there floating anymore.

Letters should be heard, they shouldn't be silent, they're the foundation of our spoken language for crying out loud. So let's assemble all the silent letters and form a new word, how about 'chashlwth'. It can be a brand new word with a dictionary definition as follows......

Chashlwth (chas-el-with) [org. fed up] **1** of too many letters **2** an overstuffed word consisting of excessive letters **3** a word with silent letters causing confusion, anger, and bitterness toward any given language **4** a word containing silent letters often used by adults or persons in a position of authority (*see* teachers) to trick young schoolchildren during spelling bee competitions causing them public humiliation in front of their family members and peers. Sometimes resulting in loss of said competition, depression, and in some cases pre adolescent suicide.

I think this could be a great idea. I appreciate you *listening* to me. I would be *honored* to *know whether* you agree. *Wrestle* with the idea a bit and let me *know* in *writing.* Because as you *know*, the pen is mightier than the *sword.*

DID YOU KNOW THAT NAMING YOUR DOG 'RAPE' IS A BAD IDEA?

It seems to be the trend these days to give things obscure and sometimes ridiculous names. Some celebrities have given their children names like Apple, Moon Unit, Dweezil, Zowie, etc. Even more alarming is the collection of silly pet names that come about, Tinkerbell, Snowpuff, Mr. Twiddles, etc. So, where do we draw the line? Is there even a line? The answer is yes. You cannot name your dog 'Rape.' It just doesn't work. You will never be able to go to the local park and throw the ball for Rape. You will never be able to toss a Frisbee and shout for your dog to return it. You will never be able to call your dog back if it starts to run away.

Standing in a crowded park filled with families and children is not the place to yell at the top of your lungs. "RAPE… RAPE! RAAAAPPPPPPEEEEE!!!

Praise is something that all healthy dogs need, it enforces the bond between dog and owner. There is no way you can be out in public with your dog and as it obeys a command you say loudly" Good Rape, what a good Rape". And creepier yet you can not do it in that half whisper half baby talk voice that all dog owners break into when they talk to their mutt's. Stick with a name like Bingo or Rex or even Fluffy, but don't ever walk your dog and with a big smile utter, "I sure do love my Rape. What would I ever do without my furry little Rape"?

CHAPTER EIGHT

YOU'RE IN THE ZONE KID!

WOW! You are really in the zone. You made it this far and I can only assume that it means you're intrigued. And if you're intrigued that means you must be letting your fabulous mind open up a wee bit. That's great! Are you starting to see that all the things I'm saying are true? That they've been right there in front of you your whole life and you overlooked them. It's incredible isn't it? I know, who would have believed it? And we still have much more to go. As a little reward for your dedication, patience, and openness, I give to you a free picture of a steel girder. That's from me to you at no charge. It's my little way of rewarding you, saying "Way to go! Good for you little fella or girl."

STEEL GIRDER

Take just a few minutes and absorb your free girder. Enjoy it. Take a rest from reading for a while. Take a few deep breaths as you look at the lovely girder. Do some stretches, crack your neck, fart.

Okay, good. Now that you've had a well-deserved break, let's move on. You can come back and look at the girder whenever you want once we've finished the book.

DID YOU KNOW THAT MARTIN LUTHER KING HAD ANOTHER DREAM?

History tells us that there are too few GREAT human beings in this world, but no one would argue that Dr. Martin Luther King Junior is near the top of the list. The dynamic and impassioned civil rights leader laid down his life in the name of a higher cause. He gave everything in the name of freedom. His life was spent ensuring that the ones that came after him would have a better life. A life of dignity, equality and true freedom. Who can ever forget Mr. King's incredible speeches? His poignant insights and observations? Who can forget his most memorable phrase, *"I have a dream!"* Indeed the good doctor did. He had a dream of climbing to the mountain top and looking down on a world where every man woman and child were equal and one. Brothers and sisters despite race, religion, color or creed. What a mighty, mighty dream. But did you know that Martin Luther King had another dream?

It went like this. He dreamt of a yellow ostrich floating around in the sky. Mr. King jumped to the ostrich and they floated over an ocean filled with jellybeans. Suddenly the ostrich turned into president Nixon and they turned upside down and played chess in a barn. As Dr. King tried to talk to Mr. Nixon, Mr. Nixon turned into some unknown kid with red hair, braces and freckles. They now stood at the edge of a field and the kid started to cry. Mr. King consoled the stranger and went and got him some leather couches. But when he returned with the couches Sylvester Stallone was riding a magic seahorse. Mr. King turned and ran but suddenly he was surrounded by walls, giant hundred foot walls crawling with spiders and popcorn. Mr. King screamed and the walls fell down only to reveal he was standing in the mouth of a giant sea turtle. Mr. King started to talk, his voice echoing, suddenly he broke into a full soprano opera voice and sang at the top of his lungs. Lights came up in the turtle and an audience filled with unicorns in suits and ties were applauding wildly. One of them charged the stage and started kissing Dr. King passionately and…. That's when Mr. King finally woke up.

Everybody has more than one dream. Man, dreams are weird aren't they?

DID YOU KNOW THAT CHEERIOS COULD BE USED AS LIFE RAFTS?

Saving lives is a serious matter. Every year thousands of lives are lost to drowning. Millions of lives if you count ants. Yes, we've all seen it. You're swimming around in a crystal clear pool on a gorgeous summer day and as you tread water you notice something on the waters surface.

Of course there's the odd leave or a pine needle or some debris, but what's harder to see are little, brown ants. So tiny and fragile, these little fellahs can be plucked off the ground by the slightest breeze. Their bodies so light that they can become airborne from a sneeze. Well, what goes up must come down, and sadly, very often the little brown ants come down in the swimming pool.

Their legs are so tiny they can't swim, their bodies so insignificant they cant sink. So what do they do? They float. They float and float for hours and days, the life slowly being drained from them as they lay helpless in a backyard pool that to them must seem like the Atlantic Ocean.

So, what does one do to put a stop to the madness? How do you play lifeguard to an ant? Easy, you go in the house, grab a box of whole wheat Cheerios and start tossing the Cheerios into the pool like little, tiny, ant personal floatation devices. I know that we're talking about a breakfast cereal here, but we're also talking about millions of lost lives. It's okay to be innovative. We must help the ants survive. I mean who else is going to eat the dollops of raspberry jam we spill on our kitchen counters. Throw the Cheerios in your pool and be supportive and encouraging as the ants grab hold and struggle toward the edge of the pool. "Swim little felah's swiiiimmmm! If you start to lose energy bite into your life raft! It contains niacin, thiamin, riboflavin, and 12 other essential vitamins to start your day. *Swiiiiiiiimmmmmmmmm!!!!"*

DID YOU KNOW THAT EGGS ARE UNBORN BABIES?

How many eggs do you eat in a year? Hundreds I'm sure. Scrambled, fried, over easy, poached, boiled, etc. Fine, and at the same time, how dare you!

Has it ever occurred to you exactly what eggs are? They are little unborn chickens. Yes, that's right, unborn chickens. Does that not make you want to stop and give pause for just a moment. Of course we all love a good omelett, but do we love it enough to make it with the whipped bodies of dead babies? Eggs are like external wombs or port-a wombs if you will. Instead of the baby growing inside the mother it grows in this nifty, convenient, port-a womb. But before the babies have a chance to emerge and run and play and chirp, we throw them into a frying pan. Good God in heaven. When you want a burger you don't pull the calf from the cows belly and eat it. When you want bacon or goat cheese you don't dine on unborn barnyard animal fetus. So why do we eat eggs? What are we lizards? By all that's holy, what are we doing? Can't we let the baby chicks at least hatch and then scramble them up? We boil lobster, why not baby chicks? I'm just saying there has to be a more humane way to eat birds.

DID YOU KNOW THAT STUFFING YOUR MATRESS WITH RICE KRISPIES WILL HELP YOU SLEEP?

Having trouble sleeping at night? Tossing, turning, counting sheep? Nothing can be more torturous than laying in the dark and your eyes wont shut. No matter what you do you can't fall asleep. Sleeping pills, aromatherapy, soft music, recordings of waves or birds singing, nothing seems to work. At long last I offer the solution. It's safe, cheap, and easy. All you need to do is stuff your mattress with Rice Krispie cereal by Kellogs. Fill that mattress right to the top. Now lay back down and slowly, purposely, pee the bed. Within seconds you will start to hear the trademark sounds 'snap, crackle, pop.' It's the noise that made the cereal famous. Within minutes the soothing rhythm of this crispy sound will gently lull you into a deep and deserved sleep.

Like the crickets rhythmic song, lightly chirping on a balmy summers eve, the 'snap, crackle, pop,' will help you drift away into a soft, sustained slumber for hour after glorious hour. At last when you awake the next day, just get up from your urine soaked mattress, stretch, go to the shower and wash the stale pee off your body, dress, and start your day, fresh as a daisy.

DID YOU KNOW THAT 7-11 CONVENIENCE STORES COULD HAVE JUST BEEN CALLED 18?

I'm not sure who comes up with the names for things but it occurred to me that there seems to be a lot of waste. 7-11 for example, a place that we've all frequented when in need of a Hostess Ho Ho or an AquaSplash Gatorade or a condom. Here is a place with two numbers in its name, seven followed rather quickly by an eleven. Okay, fine, catchy, it even rhymes, but honestly, couldn't they just have saved a number and called the damn place Eighteen? I mean Seven Eleven doesn't even make sense. What does it mean? We're open seven days a week eleven days of the year? Huh? It's not the hours because it's open twenty four hours a day so then it would have to be called Twenty Four Seven, in which case I again would argue why not just call it Thirty One and save on numbers?

The other thing that team Seven Eleven failed to take into account is that Seven Eleven can obviously be misconstrued as a math problem and not a convenient place to stop and get sour cream and onion Pringles. Most folks aren't good at mathematics or have the time or inclination for it, so why taunt people with something they don't desire. I know it's too late now, but for future reference for all those involved in the "naming things" business, try to minimize numbers words and space. It would make it all so much easier on the rest of us. Ok, got it? Ten-four good buddy.

DID YOU KNOW THAT TOO MANY CEILING FANS COULD CAUSE YOUR HOUSE TO FLY AWAY?

Summer can be the most beautiful time of the year but also the most miserable. No one likes to suffer through the stifling heat and the horrid humidity. The only respite is the cool interior of an air-conditioned car or building, or the gentle breeze offered by a ceiling fan. For many people central air conditioning is a costly proposition. The economically sound alternative is a series of strategically placed ceiling fans throughout ones home. One or two seem to be adequate. Any more than that and one is most certainly flirting with disaster.

It is obvious that ceiling fans are nothing more than spinning propellers hanging overhead. Their basic design is not that dissimilar to the rotors on an average helicopter. Well, we all know the results helicopters achieve when their rotors pick up enough speed and torque. The choppers become airborne.

It is based on the simple laws of physics that I encourage you not to A: Install more than three ceiling fans. B: Not to do the wiring yourself. Spend the extra money and hire a skilled and competent electrician. And C: Do not turn the fans to full power in unison. The following outcome will result. Your house will become airborne. It will slowly lift from its foundation and before you can run out the front door to get help you will already be floating high above your town or city. Unless you have a passion for doing traffic reports or covering high-speed chases from the comfort of your own home, I suggest you follow my advice and stick to the rules I've outlined above. I especially don't recommend you go to bed with all the ceiling fans activated. It is a rude awakening when one gets up in the morning, goes to the front door to retrieve the morning paper, opens the door and looks down to see Greenland thousands of feet below. Be smart, be cool, and follow my rule.

DID YOU KNOW THAT COBBLER IS MADE OUT OF COBBLER?

Who doesn't love a nice bowl of cobbler? Apple, cherry, blueberry? Mmmmmmmmmmm, what a tasty treat. Hold it! Wait just one second. You know who *doesn't* enjoy a bowl of cobbler? Cobblers, that's who.

Does no one else find it odd that the title of a shoe repairman's job is on menus across America? Something is afoot I say. When was the last time you broke a shoe or wore out a heel? It happens now and again. So, where do you go, a shoe repair right? Except not too long ago we called them cobblers. Not any more. When was the last time you heard someone say, " Honey call the cobbler my sandal strap snapped, or, Darling, do we have the number of a good cobbler, my loafer needs new stitching. You'd have as much luck hearing someone call for a blacksmith or a town crier.

So what happened to cobblers? Where did they go? It seems to me we still have a function for them. We all wear out our shoes eventually. So how is it they vanished like the wooly mammoths after the last ice age? And how is it we conveniently have a dessert called 'COBBLER'?

You don't have to be on CSI or be buddies with Hannibal Lecter to figure this one out. Cobblers are cobbler and are being eaten as desserts all across the country, and they have been for many years.

These poor craftsmen were silently fazed out of society and the workplace in a move so subtle yet so clever it's almost hard to believe. But believe it we must and credit must go to the mastermind who conceived the idea of eliminating cobblers by grinding them up and putting them in the oven. Simply hide the taste of human flesh with a thick, brown sugar topping and no one will be the wiser. And the plan might have worked except for one dead giveaway clue. They named the damn dessert after the victims. You never see 'banker' or 'chiropractor' on the dessert menu, so why did they think we would be so stupid as to not link the slow disappearance of cobblers to the irresistible dessert know as cobbler found on menu's in fine restaurants everywhere? We're not that dumb. Just remember, next time you order cobbler your not just eating a scrumptious dessert, you're eating an occupation.

DID YOU KNOW THAT ESKIMO'S CAN LICK HOUSES DOWN?

Igloos have to be one of the most interesting yet confusing structures know to man. The idea of keeping yourself sheltered from snow, ice, and sub zero temperatures by building a house of ice is borderline scandalous.

Imagine being freezing cold and as a remedy you step into a cold shower, huh? How does this make sense? Talk about reverse psychology. The Eskimos have done it to mother nature.

With meticulous precision Eskimos carve blocks of snow from the ground and layer them one on top of the other to make domed shelters out on the ice shelves. These ingenious structures keep them safe and warm and appear to be quite cozy. So successful are these tiny buildings that whole communities of them spring up across the endless snow plains of Eskimo country. But where there's communities there's neighbors, and where there's neighbors there is always bound to be conflict. The rule is no different with Eskimos. There are obviously going to be scenarios where one Eskimo's seal blubber is too close to the other Eskimo's home, or a sled dog is barking all night and no one can sleep. How about a careless neighbor leaving his harpoons lying about or his smoked salmon wafting in your igloo window? The point is there's a whole myriad of problems that go on in Eskimo country.

In cases where these conflicts are not settled amicably it can get real ugly real fast. One of the big problems of living in a house made of snow is its susceptibility to permanent damage or destruction. Feuding Eskimos have been know to sneak over to another Eskimo's domicile in the middle of the night and slowly, quietly, lick it down. Yes, using nothing more than their tongues these skilled nomads have perfected the art of licking down an annoying neighbors igloo before they can wake up and know what has happened. In other circumstances, Eskimo neighbors have been so enraged that sometimes an Eskimo family will wake up and find their house to be yellow. Clearly this is not acceptable. Eskimos either have to learn to live more harmoniously or they're going to have to invest in building materials that don't melt or stain with urine so very easily.

DID YOU KNOW THAT I JUST SPELLED 'KNOW' WITH A ZERO?

I don't like to be deceitful; God knows we live in a society that's filled with enough con-artist's. But did it ever occur to you that you might have been conning yourself and others since the day you learned how to spell? Case in point, what I am about to type is the letter o, 'O', there it is, plain and simple. Now, I am about to type the number zero, 'O' there it is. Now, you tell me the difference? You can't can you? Do you realize that for most of your life you've been writing with a number? That's not exactly honest now is it? No it is not. Zeros and O's have made liars out of all of us. You'd think with all the variations on lines available to us, with the plethora of graphic designers and the broad scope of the human imagination we could have come up with a more unique design for at least one of these symbols. Would it have not been easy to give the zero a cross like the 't' has, or a dot, like the 'i'? Maybe we could have bent it in a little at the sides so it looked like it had hips, something.

We don't use other numbers in our spelling. Tonight isn't spelled 2night, but if it were at least it would be more honest than spelling 'zoo'. Is it 'zoo', or is it z-zero-zero? How can we know? Lets keep some separation here for god sakes, I mean what's next, a sentence that reads like this?

" I ruined a 1derful day by 4getting my 10iss racket. I h8te when that happens."

It's up to you people. Continue to lie to everyone by using zero's in your spelling, or come clean and put little arrows by all your O's with a caption that says 'This is a lie'.
(see diagram below)

Hello, it's very nice to see you.

THIS IS A LIE   **THIS IS A LIE**   **THIS IS ALSO A LIE**

CHAPTER NINE

FUNGUS IS NO FUN, GUS!

Let's talk about fungus. Do we all know what fungus is? It's the stuff that looks like a mushroom but grows on the sides of trees. Fungus usually grows on old, damp, rotten surfaces. Do you have fungus on your brain? It's possible. And here's why. Your brain is a machine, much like a car engine or a generator or a popcorn popper. In order for that machine to function it needs to run. If it doesn't run it gets lethargic and cranky, slow and unreliable. In essence, it can start to go numb. You ever hear the Pink Floyd song 'Comfortably numb?' If not it's worth a listen, the words are impactful.

"When I was a child I caught a fleeting glimpse, out of the corner of my eye. I turned to look but it was gone. I cannot put my finger on it now. The child is grown, the dream is gone. I have become comfortably numb."

The song will possibly reflect on you on how you have allowed your life to become comfortable, safe, and filled with patterns of predictability. You've let your imagination, openness and childish curiosity disappear. Sometimes it's easier just to coast, not tax ourselves, know what we know and just leave it at that... and that attitude my friends is when the fungus starts to grow.

You mustn't let your mind go stagnant. You mustn't allow your mind to go on vacation or take time off. Keep it working, keep it thinking, exploring, and wondering. That's what it wants, that's what it needs. Don't let the machine get gunked up. Keep the pistons firing on all chambers. Allowing yourself to become comfortably numb is no fun Gus. So keep on thinking. Keep on reading. Take in the new thoughts, inspirations and ideas. Feel the machine!

DID YOU KNOW THAT GLOBAL WARMING COULD BE REDUCED IF WE ALL LEFT OUR FRIDGES OPEN?

As the doomsday of global warming approaches, we as a species must be afraid. It is in that fear that the human race will get off its duff and become proactive about saving planet Earth, the place we call home.

Everybody knows by now that all our human activity is taking a massive toll on our planet. Our fragile ecosystem is being eaten away faster than acne eats away at a teenagers face and ass. The planet is warming up folks. We're using too much energy and emitting to many high levels of toxicity into the air. Sure we can all cut back here and cut back there, but in the end it's a fools practice. We are human with everyday human needs. We all need to flush the toilet, heat our homes, start our cars, build our buildings, eat our crops. It is pessimistic yet certain reality to think that we can stop or even slow down the snowball of need and consumption that we have given birth to. Even environmentalist and the Greenpeacers have to fuel themselves. The Rainbow Warrior doesn't run on magic rainbow crystals, it chugs across the ocean on the same damn oil that the whaling boats they are chasing spew into the sea.

We can't all stop what we are doing, we're a machine, a living force, a parasite on the back of Earths neck, and we are killing it just by living. With a population of six billion ready to double and then triple within the next century what are we to do to save ourselves? How do we stop the warming that we are causing? How do we stop everything from melting? How can we throw this killer process into reverse and cool things down?

Easy… everyone leave his or her fridges open. Turn on your air conditioners and ceiling fans and leave all your doors and windows open. We all love to be in a comfort zone. Nothing feels better than a temperature controlled room. If we all do our part and let the frosty air from our fridges spill out into the atmosphere and allow the frigid blast of our air conditioners to carry out into the streets of our cities then we'll all be doing our part. It's not that hard to figure out. So take a break from reading and go and throw your refrigerator and freezer doors wide open. Put the air conditioner on full, open all the doors and windows in your house and start doing your part to save our planet. It's no longer a question of "Should I?" It is now a statement where you say "I must."

DID YOU KNOW THAT SKUNKS SHOOT ASS SAUCE?

Many of us have been attacked by an animal, bit by a dog, scratched by a cat, chased by a rhino, swooped by a grackle, lunged at by a bear or a squirrel, and it's never a pleasant experience. It can often leave us bloodied and bruised, frightened and scarred, emotionally as well as physically.

Animals use their superior strength to overpower us or in some cases their pointed teeth or razor sharp claws. Smaller animals can be just as lethal as larger ones using defense arsenals that range from toxic poisons to lethal stings. But there is one animal in the animal kingdom that perhaps deals the most lethal blow of all. It is a small animal that leaves a giant sized scar in the wake of its unorthodox attack. I am talking about the skunk. A solitary animal that scavenges for food in the alleyways and backyards of our communities. This nocturnal hunter does not invite confrontation but in the event of it can leave us feeling humiliated, smelly and alone. Unlike any other critter in the animal kingdom, the skunk will defend its personal space by raising its tail, puckering its anus, and squirting a facefull of ass sauce right between your eyes. Like a Discovery Channel enema gone wrong, this vile fluid will project itself ten to twenty feet to find its mark. It is clear that skunks must spend a great portion of their lives doing rectal exercises. The power and accuracy of their ass sauce blasts is unprecedented anywhere else in the universe. Not even after a night of bad sushi could us humans hold a candle to the ass-squirting prowess of the small but mighty skunk.

So, humans be warned, next time you take a leisurely evening stroll, you are leaving yourself open and vulnerable to a face full of the skunk's homebrewed ass Gatorade.

Be smart, wear a goalie mask and carry lots of tomato juice. It may be the only way to survive.

DID YOU KNOW THAT IF Russell Crowe, Ethan Hawke, Dan Quail, Sheryl Crow, and Steven Seagal ALL GOT TOGETHER THEY WOULD TECHNICALLY BE A FLOCK OF BIRDS?

Imagine if you will, a nice fall day, the sky crisp and clear. As you look overhead you see a spot on the horizon. As the spot gets closer you recognize the unmistakable flapping of wings and realize that there is a flock of birds heading in your direction. Geese? Pelicans? Sparrows? What would you say if I said celebrities?

As the flock comes into plain sight you now begin to see details, and sure enough, high above your head is a traditional V formation with several famous people flapping overhead. Dan Quail, our former

Vice President, Ethan Hawke, man/boy movie star, Steven Seagal, former action star and ponytail perpetuator, Top recording artist Sheryl Crow, and brooding leading man Russell Crowe. With all their last names ending with a bird name they legally have the right to form a flock and fly south when the notion hits them.

Now, why these gentlemen and lady have bird names is not known. What is known is that they are all strong fliers and seem to be aeronautically sound. All we can do is wave to them as they gracefully fly past and wish them a safe and pleasant journey. May they arrive in one piece at their magical tropic climes and enjoy many a breathtaking sunset on the warm beaches of paradise. And let's pray that none of these gifted celebrities fly into giant, energy generating wind mill.

DID YOU KNOW THAT IF YOU DON'T MILK COWS THEY GO SOUR?

The smell of sour milk is enough to make one vomit. Consuming a mouthful of dated milk is a mistake we all make at least once in our lifetimes. It is both foul and nauseating. Milk is one of the few beverages we use that has a short shelf life. If not consumed within a two-week period it starts to turn. The reason may seem scientific and the answer may have to do with bacteria and mold and so forth, but the true cause of souring milk comes straight from the source, cows!

Cows create milk, we all know this. Farmer's milk the cows, we all know this as well. But did you ever stop to ask, why do they milk them? What is the purpose? Well, the answer is easy. If we don't milk the cows, they to will go sour. Their innards are floating in fresh dairy milk. The only way to get it out of their systems is to have someone slowly and delicately tug on their teaks. If this practice is not preformed within a suitable period of time the milk will curdle and a perfectly good cow will go sour.

Our symbiotic relationship with cows helps us enjoy nourishing and vitamin enriched milk, while at the same time ensuring the continuation of an important domesticated species. The option to this give and take method of survival is thus. We humans would drive through the countryside only to see expired cows now laying as blobs of cottage cheese with horns sticking out of them. Vast fields of prime grazing grass would be littered with these unfortunate beasts that couldn't find anyone to suck on their teats. Thank goodness for our never-ending appetite for dairy goods, and thank god for the gentle, milk giving beast we know as the cow.

DID YOU KNOW YOUR MINI VAN IS RUNNING ON TRICERATOPS?

Willy Nelson has a tour bus that runs on vegetable oil. He stops at diners and fast food outlets along his tour route and attains their used vegetable oil. Sound funny? Well you might want to think twice before you start laughing at the old yellow bearded crooner. Because believe it or not, your vehicle is running on T-rex and Ankylosaurus right now.

Remember the other night when you ran out to dinner and a movie? Or hauled the kids off to soccer practice? Guess what, you got there on velocoraptor fumes. The gasoline and oil that run your vehicle are made from crude. And where does that come from? Under the earth. Pockets of trapped gas and oil are the byproduct of decomposed and petrified plant and animal life that went through a long geologic process that I wont bore you with right now. What I can say is that these liquefied corpses are at this very moment sloshing around in your gas tanks and fueling your Volkswagen, Porsche's and Dodge Neon's.

That's right people, you're not running on miles per gallon, you're running on miles per Brontosaurus. "Fill her up with Stegosaurus Percy, and while you're at it look under the hood and make sure my terradactyl isn't getting low." Who knew that something as modern as the car, the jet, the space shuttle, were running on something older than time itself. How many of you were aware that ancient dinosaurs were still truly running the earth?

DID YOU KNOW THAT BLACK PEOPLE AREN'T BLACK?

Now wait a second! Before ya'll go getting your ginch in a blender, let me explain. Think about it? Take a look at the color black, pure black. Look around wherever you may be and find something black. Stare at it a minute, examine it, take it all in. Black, black, black…. Good, now ask yourself if you ever in your life have seen someone who's black? The answer is no! No one is *black.* The people we refer to as black aren't black at all, they're brown. Some are light brown, some are dark brown, some are very dark brown, but never have I seen a human being who is truly black. The closet I've seen is maybe some Kenyan's or other tribal people from Africa, but no person of color is pure black. In fact as far as color goes there are some, including scientists and artists that claim black is officially not a color at all. Some theorize when there is no light then there are no photons of light, which means there are no photons of color, so black cannot be a color.

By calling a people black are we calling them nothing? What if the first person to ever label an African was not good with color or color blind? He or she called them black but was wrong, yet somehow the label stuck? The truth is, if anything, black people should be called brown. Wouldn't that be more accurate? Somebody somewhere obviously made a mistake. Let's change it. In fact let's change things across the board. White people aren't white, we're a light pink, possibly even a mild rose'. Asian people aren't yellow. The Simpson's are yellow, Asians are just kind of pale, probably more white than us pinks. And Indians, red? I don't think so. How about a beautiful mild bronze. You know who's red, the devil and embarrassed people that's who. We should all be embarrassed for creating this abysmal human color chart. It is grossly inaccurate. If it were a paint store it would have been shut down years ago. To all my brown, pink, pale, and bronze friends, and anyone else who has been falsely branded a skin color, I say rejoice in who you really are. Claim your color and wear it proudly...... except for the green people, Hulk, Li'l Green Sprout, Shrek, and the Green Giant, never really liked the greenies, they scare me.

DID YOU KNOW THAT LASAGNA CAN PROTECT YOU FROM RE-ENTRY INTO THE ATMOSPHERE?

We all have the need for speed. Who amongst us can say we haven't put the pedal to the metal and wailed down the highway in the family car? There's an exhilarating rush one gets as the dormant world whizzes by. There's a sense of dominance over the universe, a feeling of power and control. But rare is the individual who has truly pushed the limits of their vehicle to its full potential. Are we scared of too much speed? The answer is yes.

Too much speed can lead to an unmanageable situation. Air friction can cause our vehicles to overheat and in time explode. We're all familiar with the grim fate of some of our space shuttles. Sadly, some of them did not survive the rigors of space, and one in particular did not survive the 3000 degree Fahrenheit heat generated at reentry into earth's atmosphere. But, despite all that tragedy, humans continue to be risk takers and thrive on pushing the boundaries of what we can achieve.

It therefore makes sense that humans want their vehicles to attain maximum power to the point of breaking through the sound barrier. Mini vans and the like deserve to get to where they need to go at breakneck speed. So how, realistically, do we protect our precious cargo, our family? How can we ensure they are not devoured in a ball of flame when we hit mach 2 or 3?

The space shuttle's solution is a series of small, specially fabricated ceramic tiles that deflect and absorb heat. They are affixed to the exoskeleton of the wings and fuselage and successfully keep the interior of the shuttle cooled. That's the good news. The bad news is that each of these tiles costs an estimated four thousand dollars apiece and it would take a hundred or more to cover our cars and mini vans. So, what's the average consumer and soccer mom and dad to do?

The answer surprisingly comes from Italy. The Italians conceived of a delicious noodle dish called lasagna. Unknowingly they cut it into traditional squares that just happen to be the exact dimensions of the expensive space tiles. With a tray of lasagna costing a few mere dollars to prepare, it now becomes feasible for us citizens to jump into the speed game with a cost effective alternative to NASA's highly successful space tile.

In the span of an afternoon it is possible to cover your vehicle with squares of lasagna and safe-proof your recreational vehicle against the ravages of re-entry.

With a full on ground beef, ricotta cheese, and tomato sauce base serving as insulation, you can now drive at top speeds with the comfort of knowing an absorbent pasta shell is protecting you and your loved ones. The faster you drive the sooner your vehicle fills with the delicious aroma of slow cooking lasagna. Happy travels and watch out for children crossing the galaxy.

DID YOU KNOW THAT YOU CANT THROW AWAY A GARBAGE CAN?

Some things in life are just impossible to do. Case in point, throwing away a garbage can. Like all materials, garbage cans do have a shelf life. They get thrown around, bruised and battered and over time become victim to wear and tear. They incur damages and eventually are no longer functional. So, like all unwanted things we come to a point in time where we have to throw it out. But have you ever tried throwing away a garbage can? It doesn't work. You take it down to the edge of the curb and you stand it next to the other garbage cans. You can't put it in the other garbage cans because it's the same size, it won't fit. The only choice is to stand it along side. So now, when the garbage man comes he can just throw it away right? Wrong! He just thinks it's another garbage can, and what's more he's happy about the can because he notices that it's empty and it's one less heavy can filled with all your junk that he doesn't have to lift.

So what do you do? Nothing really. You just have to keep using your garbage can over and over until finally it gets blown away in a wind storm, or a neighbor steals it, or a flash flood carries it off to the sea. Throwing a garbage can in the garbage is like trying to remove the wet from water. It cannot be done. I have been trying to throw one of my garbage cans away for fourteen years. It is useless. It can't be done.

CHAPTER TEN

WOW! LET'S TAKE A BREAK.

Wheeeeeeew... you've come a long way. You're brain must be pounding. So much new information, so much fresh knowledge. I bet you feel good though, don't you? I bet you feel like there's a bit of a new bounce in your step, a new inner confidence, a little razzamatazz! Hey, I'm not surprised. That's what happens when you get new knowledge, it just feels good. It's like the first time you put on new shoes or socks or a dress or a shirt. It's like that first time you feel a brand new pair of undies rub up against your sex machine. It just makes you feel better.

On the same note we have to be careful not to overindulge. Make sure your cup don't runneth over. Pacing is imperative. It would be foolhardy to blaze through all this new information only to realize you absorbed too fast and you now have an aneurism. This book shall not, I repeat, *SHALL NOT* be the cause of loss of human life. To ensure this we're going to slow down a little. The next page is like a little naptime. As you will see there is nothing on it. Most books are so busy shoving words in your face they don't realize that people need to stop and take a breath. You don't work non-stop, or swim or golf of sleep or do anything without some kind of break, so why not here? I want you to turn to the next page and enjoy the blankness. Stare at it. Stare into it. Start drooling, allow your eyes to glaze over, zombify yourself. Just relax, maybe even visualize your own NEW idea. Maybe even scribble it into the blankness with a pen, lip liner, or a piece of charcoal that you find. But most of all just take a break.

I really mean it. I want you to stare at the empty page for a minimum of three minutes and see if something comes into your head. It is my hope that your brain is so hopped up on the new openness you have found that it has become infectious. That in the blankness your brain will have a run on effect from these pages and you will concoct your own *new* concept, idea, or fact that has been in front of you your whole life. Don't be afraid. Stare at the blankness and let your mind breathe. Let your mind shed all convention, all the rules of education, society, and familiarity. Let your damn mind go free, just for three minutes. Take the budgie out of the birdcage and hold it up to the sky. Open your hands and set it free. You can do it, I know you can, because you're the budgie man! You're the godforsaken, "set the budgie free man..." what do you see? Be free! What do you see?

Okay, so how was it? Did you see anything in the blankness? Did your mind roam free or were you busy thinking about how you might feel foolish? Stupid? Insane? Those are excuses. Shallow reasons to not participate in newfound stimuli. You want to try again? Go on back a page and don't cheat yourself of the blankness. Honest to god, don't be such a coward? Are you afraid you might have an erratic thought? A nonsensical idea? A genius moment? There's no rules. Nobody has control over how you think or what you think. Go back a page and try again if you just went on past. Don't shortchange yourself. Stop caring about what others might think if they happen to look over and see you staring at a blank page, it could be fun.

The following is a true story. Something I did when I was younger and still working at a boring nine to five day job.

I used to have to take buses and subways around town to get to work everyday. It was miserable. The worn down and lost faces of other commuters made me feel as if I was riding on the train of the dead. People's faces had the look of lost souls. It was tragic, but I don't begrudge those people, like me, they were eking out an honest living. I would get so bored on my daily trips I would often imagine strange and obscure things to help me pass the time. One day on my journey home I carried with me a hardbound book with nothing but blank pages. I don't remember where I got it but it was lying around at the office somewhere. Maybe it was a sketchbook or something, but each page was as empty as a field of snow. As I sat at the back of the bus, bored beyond tears, I decided to have a little fun. Surrounded by other commuters I opened the book to the middle and pretended to start reading it. I used my finger to follow lines that weren't even there. I made my lips move in silence as if I were reading actual words to myself. I tilted the book down so that people around me were able to see that there was no writing on the pages. I can only imagine what must have been running through their heads. I kept a straight face and often looked up from the page as if I was deep in thought, contemplating what I just read. Or from time to time I would emit a soft chuckle and shake my head as if I had just digested a clever or witty paragraph.

It wasn't long until people around me started to take notice. Their reactions were all internal and their eyes gave away a sense of bewilderment, shock, and confusion. I felt empowered. Here I was doing next to nothing out of the ordinary. Acting out a common sight right before the public's eyes. For all intensive purposes, I was reading. The only difference was that there were no words, but the actions were exactly the same. Yet somehow I had captivated an audience, I had given them something to think about on their ritual commute of mind numbness. I had thrown them an innocent curveball that put some stimulus into their otherwise death train ride home.

Did they feel angst, danger, curiosity, fear? Who knows? The point is that it didn't take much for me to feel alive by offering them an alternative to what their minds had been programmed to know. And by me feeling alive, they in turn felt more alive wondering how a seemingly average man could be reading a book with no words.

Have you ever tried something you wouldn't normally try? Have you ever done something different that might have an effect on others? Maybe it's time to try. Maybe it's time to imagine. If you're out in public, at an airport or a coffee shop, anywhere where there are people around, try turning this book upside down for a few minutes. Pretend you're reading it just as normal. Look around and see if you catch someone's eye. If you do just keep on holding the book upside down and pretend you're reading like everything is normal. Sneak a peek and take in the onlooker's faces. Be sure not to break your focus and give in to fear. Keep the book upside down and absorb the way you feel as others try to deal with the confusion and their own discombobulation.

I bet you'll feel yourself smiling inside. You'll strangely enough feel empowered. I'm not sure why, but I think it comes from the gratitude your brain is sending, saying, "thanks! Thanks for bending the rules a little bit. Thanks for being creative and silly. Thanks for trying something new."

I hope you have the courage and the fun within you to try this little exercise. It will truly help you physically understand the idea of things not always having to be what they seem. When you finish having fun turn this book back over the right way and we'll continue on exposing you to new things.

CHAPTER ELEVEN

$E=Mc^2$

Isn't it odd that one day a man named Albert Einstein came up with an equation that changed the world? At some point his brain just went, "Here's a thought, E=Mc2, huh!" How many billons of thoughts happen around the globe, everyday? What do you think about? Probably the stuff in your life, home, family, work, sports, money, furniture.

Later today or tonight when you're lying in bed or sitting on your couch, somewhere quiet and peaceful, I want you to purposely think of something that you normally wouldn't. A starfish, a volcano, an Australian, a desert, a tractor gear. Take something totally obscure and just let it dominate your brain for just two minutes. Picture all the things you could do with a tractor gear. Where it can go, where it's been, how it was made. Picture yourself dancing with it, flying on it, having eyes and a face, picture eating it with mashed potatoes and gravy. In other words take your mind to a place it's never been or wouldn't normally go. Let it think of something far beyond the scope of your normal logic. See what happens, Anything? Nothing? Does this one thought progress into something meaningful? Is it stimulating? Fun? Does it lead to anything meaningful? Does it open a portal in your head that had never been opened? Does it make you want to think of other strange things? Maybe, maybe not. Maybe it's a waste of time and you'll never do it again, or maybe it was refreshing and you've now decided you need to think of things other than the old familiar stomping grounds.

Hmmmmmmmm, I wonder what Albert was thinking when he thought 'energy equals mass times the velocity of light squared?' I can assure you he wasn't thinking about who was playing on Monday Night Football or his income taxes. Each human mind has the capability for it's own E=Mc2. Are you giving your mind a chance? What are you thinking about?

DID YOU KNOW THAT THREE HOUR FIRE LOGS ARE EXTREMELY INNACURATE?

I know that we live in a litigious world, and I don't want to be part of that burden on society I don't want to participate in the lawsuit happy circus that America has become, but sometimes you have to say enough is enough. If you are going to make a claim or advertise a result and you market a product that doesn't live up to that claim, it can effect your life. In fact it can ruin your life. It is my belief that in such circumstance one has to defend their rights and stand up to the corporations that often take our patronage for granted. Allow me to expand.

I am a guy who hates to wear a watch, Never liked em' never felt comfortable with them on my arm. But, in this fast paced world it is important to keep up with a demanding schedule. Meetings and phone calls, lunches and events must all be approached with a timely and professional sensibility. Obviously one needs to keep track of the time in order to manage ones affairs. How is this achieved if one is opposed to the common wristwatch? Easy, or so I thought. There is a product in the marketplace that blatantly advertises itself as an accurate timepiece. We are all familiar with the 'Three Hour Fire log.'

Its claim to telling time is right there in its title. So, as an alternative to an expensive Rolex I instead invested an equal amount of capital in crate upon crate of Three Hour Fire Logs. I thought, "how easy. A pack of matches and five logs a day and it's goodbye wristwatch." Boy, I couldn't have been more wrong. Think about it, we usually stay awake for about fifteen hours a day minimum. That works out to five, Three-Hour Fire Logs. I reasoned that by igniting my first log when I woke up and then continued lighting them on three-hour intervals throughout the day I could effectively manage my time and have successful and productive day. I would simply carry the smoldering logs in my briefcase or in my backpack and go about my business in a relaxed and orderly manner. Here's where it gets ugly. Those Three Hour Logs are about as erratic as an old lady with scorpions in her diaper. Some of them burned out way before the three hour mark and some of them burned well on into a fourth hour. Do you know how many flights I missed and how many business lunches were spoiled by these inaccurate fake lumps of timber? Yes, my life was severely affected by the false claims of the Three Hour Fire Log.

I'm hoping that justice will be served in the courtroom and my losses will be reimbursed. But more than anything I hope I win the fight to have the products name changed to Three Hour and Something Minutes Fire Log. As a footnote I am happy to say I have moved on and purchased a brand new sundial I carry with me on a piece of sod.

DID YOU KNOW THAT KOALA'S HAVE PERFECT BREAST FONDLING HANDS?

When you think of the word cute you have to think of the adorable Australian koala. What a little angel. Tufted ears, little beady eyes, that squishable face. Who on earth would not be attracted to this darling little marsupial?

As much as they are universally loved, there is one among the gender of humans who quite possibly love them more than the other. I'm talking about women. Yes there is a fondness for these little tree dwelling mammals that even surpasses men's affection for the eucalyptus-eating darlings.

Women have a secret when it comes to the mild mannered koala. They have figured out something that goes beyond cuteness and falls more into the category of koala-erotica. Yes, hard to believe, but there is an X rated factor that comes with these little bush babies that most men are oblivious to.

You see, if you study the koala's anatomy it won't take long for you to narrow in on his peculiar little hands. Slightly nubbly but able to grip the width of a mature tree quite comfortably. Also, the hand includes a stubby little thumb that supplies extra grip as it spends most of its life navigating in the precarious treetops. What women have discovered is that these same tree-climbing hands are adapted perfectly for fondling a woman's breast. The palm of the hand and strong fingers perfect for cupping a good size breast, and the nubby little thumb perfect for flicking and teasing the sensitive nipple.

Women know it takes just the right touch to have their breasts fondled successfully, and the koala has just the god given hands for the job. If you happen to hear a rustling noise coming from your girlfriends lingerie drawer, the one where she keeps sex toys and whatnot, open it slowly. It is certain that there snuggled between the undies and the vibrators you will see a loveable koala nesting in the pleasure drawer. Its wonderful breast fondling hands ever at the ready.

DID YOU KNOW THAT MEN CAN HAVE MAGIC PENIS'S?

I don't like to be that guy that exposes magic tricks but for the sake of this book I feel it is my duty. I don't know how many women have been privy to this magic trick, I don't imagine too many, but let me do my best to describe it. When a man is taking a tinkle it streams from the tip of his penis in a steady line and flows to wherever it is aimed. Sometimes, and here is the "magic" part, the flow of urine splits in the middle and magically, 'two streams' of urine occur.

Although sometimes messy, it's quite a sight to behold. So, how does this magic trick manifest? It begins in your undies.

As your undies flop around in the dryer they accumulate a certain amount of lint and or other ambiguous crusty things. Sometimes, over the course of a day or night the lint mixed with small, natural human excretions clog the eye of the penis as it lays quietly in the undies. Almost like a miniature penis beaver dam. Its not enough substance to completely plug the penis but there is enough strength in the blockage to divert the urine around it, causing the stream to divide.

The effect may only last for a few seconds, or if you're lucky maybe the duration of the whole tinkle. These are rare and should be videotaped if possible.

As I said earlier the downside is the mess. It can be hard enough to control one stream of urine, two is almost impossible. The upside, which I feel outweighs the down, is that for a brief moment in time us hard working, grown men are treated to a yellow magic show. We have a Harry Potter Penis full of mischief and wizardry. For an unexpected magic moment we are pulled back into the wonderment of childhood. A time before we had homes and mortgages, taxes and schedules. Yes, as we stand there looking down at the fantastical water show coming from between our legs we get the chance to be a kid again. I certainly hope that my expose of how the magic comes about doesn't cheapen or spoil anyone's experience. I felt it was my duty to let people in and share this often protected and private moment. I do it not to ruin the party, but instead to enlighten, and perhaps give a taste of the magic to those who have never been fortunate enough to have the blessing of a magical, double tinkle.

DID YOU KNOW THAT BLIND PEOPLE CAN READ ACNE?

It never ceases to amaze me how humans overcome incredible obstacles. Case in point, blindness. I can't imagine what it would be like to live in a life of blackness. But then again I can only imagine the richness and the depth of a blind persons imagination and the ability to paint imagery with their minds. If you are in fact blind and you are reading this book right now it is pretty much a guarantee that you are reading it in Braille. An ingenious system that allows the blind to virtually read with their fingertips. The sightless merely pass their fingers over embossed points that are arranged on a page. Essentially they *feel* the words and can read the exact things a person with sight can read. In fact it is because of this magnificent system created by Louis Braille in the 1800's that the blind can do something that no sighted person could ever achieve.

With their amazingly trained fingers blind people can caress the backs and faces of acne covered teenagers and quite literally read their bumpy skin.

Teenagers are always filled with turmoil, angst, attitude and rebellion. Their zit covered hides conceal secrets that only the blind can decipher. By slowly and carefully moving their fingertips across the skin, blind people read the story of adolescent confusion, misunderstanding, and longingness. Blind people get to look behind the door of fragile teens who are in the susceptible years proceeding adulthood.

Tragically blind people report that the story of the zit-covered teenager is always the same. After completing a reading of their pus filled welts and bumpy red skin the message always seems to read the same, "You're not getting laid until you're thirty five." Sad, but true.

DID YOU KNOW THAT PET SHOPS SELL RAW FISH CHEAPER THAN SUSHI RESTERAUNTS?

Dating can get really expensive. Taking a date to a nice restaurant can really burn a hole in your wallet. At the same time you don't want to sit at home and eat TV dinners. One of the most casual and fun dining and dating experiences can be Sushi. A culinary art form developed by the Japanese that involves the consumption of raw fish. It is surprisingly delicious and different.

The good news is that Sushi joints exist everywhere and have gained a widespread acceptance over the years. The bad news is that Sushi is easy to eat and the cost of ordering plate after plate can quickly add up. There has to be a more economic approach to eating raw fish. Thankfully there is.

As the Sushi industry has grown over the years thankfully another consumer need has flourished right along side it. Millions of people own pets. Dogs, cats, birds, hamsters etc. To service the pet industry are millions of pet shops. They have sprung up all over the country faster than breeding basset hounds. The benefit to you the consumer is also a benefit to you, the casual dater. Pet shops also carry ample supplies of live fish. Many of these fish are a delectable bite size morsel and in most cases each fish cost a fraction of the price of a single piece of sushi.

At most Pet shop outlets one can purchase a bag of two dozen goldfish for under twelve dollars. And pet shops carry exotic marine life just as diverse and varied as the Sushi joints.

Pet shops stock both fresh and salt-water varieties of fish. Imagine the delighted look on your dates face when you sit down at the next sushi restaurant and before the waiter can take your order you produce a clear plastic bag swimming with guppy's, Tetra's, Goldfish, and the always succulent Black Molly's.

You will have a limitless amount of food while maintaining your budget and enjoying the romantic ambiance of a true Sushi restaurant. You may be able to eat out twice as much as you ever have before. And the final good piece of news is this. You need not have to feel the guilt of wasting unwanted food anymore. Now, at the end of the meal you can have bonus fun by sneaking off to the bathroom together and flushing the unused part of your dinner down the toilet. The living fish actually get returned to the sea. Now that's what I call Eco-dating.

DID YOU KNOW HONKING IF YOU LOVE JESUS COULD GET YOU SENT TO HELL?

We all know that that the bible says, "Thou shalt not kill." The penalty for murder is eternal hellfire. None of us want to cross God. In fact to express our love for the lord we created an unusual form of rejoice. It comes in the form of a bumper sticker that reads as follows, *HONK IF YOU LOVE JESUS!* So what does honking and Jesus have to do with murder? It's a simple equation really. The honking of a car horn can be a startling experience for those who don't know it's coming. It is loud, unnerving, and can cause immediate distraction. In fact a loud, prolonged horn blast or even a short, abrupt horn blast can be all that's needed to frighten an unsuspecting motorist.

It is pretty much a certainty that if you honk one too many times for Lord Jesus, holy Lamb, son of our father, holy ghost and savior, that sooner or later you will frighten or distract someone to the point where they lose control of their vehicle. Just think, your symbolic honk to the Son of God just caused a housewife and her mini van full of kids to veer off into a tree. All on board are dead. Technically you become a murderer. Your weapon? Your horn and your love of Jesus. So be warned and be careful when you honk. There are not only innocent lives hanging in the balance, but there's also the destiny of your soul. Remember, horns don't kill people, Jesus kills people.

CHAPTER TWELVE

KEEP THE DRIVE ALIVE!

So, you made it this far, good for you. I hope you feel you're learning as you go. I hope your brain is pulsing and feeling alive with all the new information it's being fed. It's exciting to learn new things, It's like splashing cologne or aftershave on your face and feeling that sharp tingle, but instead you're splashing it on your brain. Does it feel all tingly and refreshing? I hope so. Life is short, so learn what you can and don't be afraid to share it with your friends and loved ones. Everyone deserves fresh information. So keep reading, there's lots more to know.

DID YOU KNOW THAT CYCLOPS'S CAN'T WINK?

It's a story as old as time, or at least as old as ancient Greece. You're sitting at a smoke filled bar, music playing in the background and suddenly from across the room you lock eyes with a complete stranger. The stranger winks at you and you are aghast. It was totally unexpected and a little presumptuous and rude. You are offended and feel a little bit violated. You turn to your friend or an associate at the bar and you say, "Hey, that creepy looking dude over there just winked at me."

You point him out in the crowd and your friend gives you a look of admonishment and says, "You idiot, he wasn't winking at you."

And you reply objectionably, "Yes he was, I saw him. He winked right at me."

Your friend rolls his eyes and responds, "The guy with the cloven feet, no shirt, scaly skin, a horn growing out of the top of his head, fur covered legs and just one eye?" "Yes, that's right."

"You mean the Cyclops?" he says almost embarrassed for you.

"If that's what he is, then yes. The Cyclops winked at me."

Your friend leans in close and talks in a hushed tone so everyone around you doesn't hear. "He's a Cyclops. He only has one eye. They can't wink. He was blinking. When you only have one eye and you blink it can sometimes look like you're winking. Got it?"

And then you get to sit there for a few minutes and feel like a complete ass. Of course, he was blinking. So you swallow your pride along with your feelings of stupidity and you have the waiter take the mythological bar hopper an exotic drink.

DID YOU KNOW THAT SOCCER BALLS ARE JUST ROLLED UP CHESS BOARDS?

Chess is a complex game. It requires skill, strategy, patience and above all a large degree of intelligence. It isn't for everyone. The combinations and patterns of complicated moves make this game not simple for the layman. People attempting to conquer the chessboard can get confused, agitated, frustrated and even angry.

It is from this anger that another game was born, a simpler game, a game for the commoner.

In the older European countries people would pass the time engaging in friendly chess matches. For the weaker players these duels often ended in tears. Their salty drops splashing all over the cardboard chessboards of the time. This liquid on cardboard dampened the chessboards considerably, making them bendable and pliable. On more than one occasion European tempers flared and a defeated player stood in anger and kicked the chessboard. Bishops and rooks flying everywhere. Well, somewhere in this tirade the airborne chessboard folded and bent and landed in a checkered clump on the ground.

Still not done with his aggression toward the board the defeated player started kicking it, causing it to take on the shape of a ball. As the tear water, dampened, board/ball, began to dry in the open sun, it started to harden. The more it hardened the farther the board could be kicked. It wasn't long until a group of angry, outdoor chess players saw the rounded board and joined in. Now a mob of unskilled chess players were chasing this rounded chess board through the streets and into fields. Some of them even bounced it up and batted it with their heads.

One in the unruly mob yelled "We hate chess! We will never ever touch it again. Only with our feet, we shall kick it in eternal punishment."

And it was on that day that the game of soccer was born. Soon teams and leauges formed. The craze caught on across Europe and the world. Dumb people everywhere were finally able to play chess in a way that made it simple.

Instead of strategically positioning an intricate army of chess pieces, now all you had to do was kick the whole chessboard into a net.

Finally the simple folk could participate in a game that was way beyond their level of comprehension. Soccer is now truly a world phenomenon. Who knows, maybe someday even a computer could play soccer.

DID YOU KNOW THAT IF YOU SHAKE CHINESE PEOPLE REALLY HARD THEY SPEAK PERFECT ENGLISH?

Mandarin is the most commonly spoken Chinese language. Over one and a half billion people speak Chinese. That's a lot of folks. It seems in today's climate Chinese is the language to learn. China is clearly an emerging economy and market. It is a sleeping giant waking up from the long winters nap of communism only to find itself stepping out into the embracing sunshine of a capitalist marketplace.

As more and more European and Western influence, money and product begin to spill over the great wall, China is now a place that everyone wants a piece of.

One of the biggest obstacles to conducting commerce with this resourceful country is the language barrier. Thousands of people are scrambling to learn Chinese. Forward thinking parents are enrolling their children in Chinese language classes. Chinese is a beautiful yet extremely intricate language. We are talking about an alphabet that has no end, where one word or letter can have multiple meanings. To those of us that don't speak Chinese the language sounds like voices from another planet. So, is there a way to speed this process up? To bridge the gap between our native tongues? Happily, the answer is a resounding, YES!

If you listen closely to someone speak in Chinese you can hear little pieces of what sound like English words or letters, but they just seem too jumbled to comprehend. The solution is this. Next time you want to speak to a Chinese person but don't have the time for a night school class, do this. As they are speaking to you, reach out and gently grab them by the shoulders. Begin shaking them very hard, sometimes violently if you have to. Within about twenty seconds you will start to hear the Chinese words begin to transgress into English words. Within about fifty seconds that Chinese person will be speaking perfectly fluent Queen's English. In fact the first words you usually hear are "Hey, why you shaking me you son of a bitch?!!"

As the world becomes closer and we all seem to have less time to get things done, this is the perfect way to overcome the problem of the Chinese language barrier.

DID YOU KNOW THAT IF YOU PULL THE LEGS OFF A FLY IT CAN'T LAND?

The common housefly is a notorious pest. Buzzing throughout our homes, crawling on our ceilings and walls, watching us with those beady Jeff Golblum like eyes. They land on our food and our skin, they dance around our faces causing us to slap futilely at the air. Their speed and agility is infamous and there is no end to the annoyance they cause to us humans.

The gift of flight is what makes them such a curse. They are next to impossible to catch and kill, so in the end they tend to have the rule of the roost in your home.

But what if we could use their very gift against them. What if we could take the mockery they make of us and turn the tables? What if flying became their worst enemy instead of their most coveted asset? Well, guess what house fly, your game is up!

One thing flies always do with certainty is buzz up against glass windows. They don't seem to get it that there is an invisible force shield between them and the outside world. Try as they might they can never penetrate the glass. Eventually they tire and have the need to rest, they have no more energy to fly. It is in this moment when the plan starts to take effect.

Simply capture the little pests between your thumb and forefinger. Gently turn them upside down and delicately pluck their hairy little legs from their torso. The fly still lives.

Once the amputations are complete, release the fly into the air and let it be free. It will instantly think it outsmarted you and circle your head as if to make a fool of you. It will perform donuts and other aeronautical feats in mid air in the center of your living room.

Eventually the antagonist will once again tire and look for a safe place to land. As it comes in for a landing it will suddenly realize it has no apparatus to grasp the wall or ceiling. It is legless! Its landing gear is gone! It can't land!

Now, at long last, you get to sit back and enjoy the show. Watch the little terror fly around in desperation, expending all it's energy, dying for a place to rest. It craves food and water to sustain its marathon flight. As an added measure of torment and cruelty, place a loaf of dog dirt on the living room floor as further torment. The fly sees the tempting loaf but can't get to the tempting loaf. It's like dangling a fat guy over an all you can eat buffet.

Yes, sometimes teasing and taunting and being a pest can come back to haunt you. In the case of the house fly lets just say us humans now have a leg up!!

DID YOU KNOW THAT POTATO SALAD HAS NO SALAD?

Talk about being sold a bad deal! How many of you have suffered the disappointment of potato salad? The word 'salad' implies lettuce does it not? How often have you sat down for a nice leafy potato salad only to find large, diced, cubes of potatoes, with virtually no lettuce leafs of any kind in sight? It's a sham. Potato salad is a lie. They even try to masquerade the potatoes under a thick, pasty mayonnaise sauce. Nice try! Potato salad my ass! It should just be called potato chunks and we just leave it at that!

DID YOU KNOW THAT WE ALL TURN INTO METEROLOGISTS IN ELEVATORS?

Being in an elevator is nothing more than being trapped in a small rectangular room pressed against countless strangers.

The room starts to move, riding between floors in an office building or an apartment or a hotel. There's nowhere to go. Nowhere to look. Nothing to say. But somehow we feel obliged to make a connection. Reach out to the other citizens of the elevator. But what can you discuss with a tiny room of total strangers that everyone will relate to? You can't bring up your love life or your gastric bypass surgery, your hemorrhoids or your in-laws, no, you need common ground. And it is then, in this unique setting that the meteorologist in all of us comes out. It's quite incredible. It's like being at a weatherman's convention except they decided to hold it in an elevator.

It usually begins with the first meteorologist/citizen saying something like, "Looks like it's real sunny out there today."

And then the next one chimes in. "Yup, gonna get real cold tonight though."

And then yet another one starts his report. "They say it's supposed to get real foggy in the morning and then a chance of showers Friday."

And then it becomes like a fever. Everyone in the elevator is a full-blooded meteorologist. "The weekends supposed to drop below freezing and there's a frost warning in effect in farm country."

It's absolutely amazing. "Yeah, that low pressure system coming in from the Maritimes is supposed to drop some of the white stuff starting early next week."

And of course there's always the hilarious elevator meteorologist who supplies the witty side note, "Hey, better get your boots on!"

And then at last the elevator doors open and like a light switch, the weather reporting stops. Almost as if they didn't want anyone to see. The meteorologist citizens pour out of the elevator and go back to being exactly who they were before they got on the elevator.

Very strange phenomenon. If you ever need to plan a vacation somewhere just step into an elevator first in order to make sure you're going to have good weather. It could mean the difference between a good holiday and a bad one.

DID YOU KNOW THAT PUTTING JUMBO SHRIMP IN YOUR BED COULD HELP EXILE AN UNWANTED LOVER?

Ever been in a situation where you can't seem to get rid of a lover, a girlfriend, a boyfriend, a one-night stand? It can be hard. Sometimes it's hard to find the words. If only there was an easier, faster, quieter method.

Well, maybe there is. Allow me to suggest a practice that's been very successful for me. After a long, wild night of steamy passion it's often hard to motivate your partner to get up and get out of your bed, or even leave your apartment. I mean, after all, you have some TV to watch. So how do you go about getting them to leave without being too rude?

Surprisingly the answer comes from the delicious world of seafood. To ensure the eviction process is successful you will need some tools. Nothing too elaborate, just a bag of frozen jumbo shrimp. Keep them on hand at all times. They will handily keep in your freezer until such time as you call on them.

Now, here's how they come into play and work as an excellent "guest remover." When you wake up in the morning don't roll over and awaken your partner. Instead, quietly sneak out of bed and collect nine or ten jumbo shrimp from the freezer. Run them under cold water for about ninety seconds to thaw. Sneak back to the bedroom, pull back the linens and liberally toss the jumbo shrimp around in the sheets. Be certain that a few of them rub up against the skin of her naked body.

Casually slide back into bed and start nuzzling her playfully.

Slowly, her adorable eyes will flutter open and her morning breath mouth will coo "Hi baby." Now it is time to go into acting mode. Pretend you have just woken up as well and respond, "Morning babe." But before she can go to kiss you with that stale, morning breath mouth, you see her eyes widen slightly as she feels something cold and clammy on her skin. You lay there acting oblivious as she starts moving around under the sheets. Her eyes filling with alarm.

Before long she nervously asks, "Do you feel something under the sheets?"

"Like what?" You ask naively.

"There's something cold and clammy rubbing up next to me. There's a whole bunch of them… ewwwww, touching my body! Like cold, dead fingers."

And that's when you look at her cool and collectively and in a calm, even voice you say, "Oh, didn't I tell you about my leprosy?"

Usually they are gone within about forty five seconds. Now it's just you, the TV, and a nice, delicious shrimp cocktail.

DID YOU KNOW THAT SNOWMEN ARE RELATED TO ANTS?

Winter wouldn't be winter without seeing a loveable snowman sitting out on someone's front lawn. These odd creatures emerge every time there's a snowfall. As quickly as they come they are just as quick to go away. But what exactly are these men made out of snow? What do we know of them? Not a lot, but we do know one thing, they are most likely the closest relative to the common ant.

The evidence is quite clear. Snowmen are a hard species to study. One, they make your fingers cold, and two, the more you touch them the more they tend to fall apart. When it gets warm they disappear altogether. What we have discovered is the obvious. Snowmen are made up of three different body parts, the base, the middle (or chest) and the head. They commonly have a rounded, bulbous shape, the head usually being the smallest part of the body and the sections getting larger as we move down to the base. In nature there is only other place where you see this configuration occur. It is the body of the ant, and some other insects like wasps, bees, or termites.

It is fortunate that snowmen only emerge in winter, a time when ants lay dormant under the ground. If ants were to ever lay eyes on their towering cousins the snowman it might well be cause for war.

Ant's are very territorial and do not like ants from other colonies close to their nests. A snowman built on the lawn where ants may be nesting could be construed as a threat. It wouldn't take long for the aggressive ants to swarm the helpless snowman and eat it alive. A fate that no one deserves. Nature seems to take care of its own, and by design, has created two species of close biological lineage that are never destined to meet.

DID YOU KNOW THAT BUBBLE GUM COMES FROM MONKEYS?

We all love chewing bubble gum. It tastes good, it smells good, and it gives us something to do with our mouths. Everybody has blown a giant pink or purple bubble that they're proud of.

Bubble gum is truly part of our culture and woven into the fabric of our lives. But where does the rubbery stuff come from? It's one of those items we take for granted and never really question.

I'll ask it again, where on earth does that stretchy, gooey, sugary treat come from? From man's closest relative that's where! I'm talking about monkeys, apes, chimpanzees, baboons, etc. Almost everything we eat comes from somewhere in nature. I mean there are a few things we create in laboratories like Twinkies and Ding Dongs but everything else has its raw materials harvested from nature. Bubble gum is no exception, and so, enter the monkeys.

We've all been to the zoo or watched Discovery channel and seen thousands of species of primates.

Going to the zoo, what an incredible way for humans to observe and learn about primates. One could stand for hours peering through the zoo glass and be mesmerized by our closest relatives, the monkey's and apes. Their every move and facial expression spellbinding.

In them we see so much of ourselves. But there is one bodily feature on these magnificent animals that cannot be ignored. Our eyes are drawn to it without fail every time. Their bright, pink and purple luminescent asses.

They stick out from the dark fur surrounding their lower extremities like a lighthouse on a foggy night.

Monkeys seem to sit a lot and so it's not until they get up and start to jump about that we see that rubbery, pink monkey ass shining in the sunlight. It looks like a giant wad of fresh bubble gum ready for the chewing.

How many of us haven't at least once had the mad desire to vault over the zoo wall and charge a monkey and just start chewing on his bubble gum ass? That enticing electric pink and purple bald patch that makes up their rear end?

It tempts us like some kind of new fantazimal candy creation from the mind of Willy Wonka himself.

"Oh, to bite into a mandrill butt and just blow a big bubble with his ass meat.

As hard as these urges are to resist, it must be twice as hard for baseball players, young children and fat people. It's surely akin to night insects drawn to the enticing purple glow of an enticing bug zapper light. Nonetheless, the bubble gum industry is huge and somewhere in a warehouse full of monkeys, somebody is carving the ass meat off a chimp so that you can blow bubbles at the ballpark with all your gum-chewing friends.

DID YOU KNOW THAT YAWNING TOO LONG COULD ALLOW A PENIS TO FLY INTO YOUR MOUTH?

Being tired can be dangerous. We've all driven our cars in an exhausted state and nodded off at the wheel. We've all just about walked into a wall because we are tired. But one of the most dangerous events by far resulting from poor sleeping habits is this. Yawning.

Not just quick little yawns. I'm talking about prolonged yawns. The ones that stretch your face to the limit and keep your mouth pulled open for a good thirty seconds. Yes, this yawn is the one to watch out for, especially in our modern, sexually charged society.

When your mouth hangs open that wide, for so long, it is truly at the mercy of the world. Anything could fly into the gaping chasm that is your mouth, a humming bird, a golf ball, or even a human cock!

Yes, I know it's startling and maybe a bit rude but this is important to know. It is not beyond the laws of reason that you could be standing on a street corner or in a mall or seated at a fancy restaurant. You lean your head back and do a full, prolonged yawn, and *WHAM!!*....

Before you know what hit you, a cock flies in your mouth. This can be a humiliating public occurrence as you fight like a marlin on a trolling rod to spit the offending phallus out of your mouth. You whip your head back and forth, side to side trying to dislodge the anonymous penis. When at last you do, the trauma is not ended. There will be nightmares and flashbacks to such a vile event. The best one can do is in the future is to take precautionary measures. The next time you yawn, for god's sake, cover your mouth! Your flattened hand makes for an excellent cock guard.

CHAPTER THIRTEEN

DON'T FEAR THE REAPER!

I'm not sure who came up with "Don't fear the reaper" but I'm guessing that the guy who did didn't have too much going on in his life. Hell's yes, you should fear the reaper. When he comes to take you away that's it, it's over. We only have one crack at the ball, one shot at life. Truth is the reaper is the *only* thing you should fear. That being said you should remember that life is a gift and should be lived to its fullest. Fear is the main reason we hold back, that we live in conformity, that we don't experiment or accept as many new things as we should. Death is final, we can't outrun death, but nothing else in life is final. We can usually find ways to alter the outcome or create a new outcome. So if death need be our only true fear, our only real fear, then there should be no fear living your everyday life. There should be no fear saying I'm going to try and attempt at least one *NEW* thing everyday or at least every week. And when I say new, that could be a new food, a new place to travel, a new type of book or genre of movie, a new person in your life, a new approach or opinion, or yes, even a new thought.

Remember, this book is about things you didn't know. At the beginning of this book did you think it would be possible to fill so many pages? Maybe you thought you already knew what I was going to say. But isn't it great that all these pages later your head has been injected with fresh information?

But maybe there's a bigger question at play here, let's put aside what I've been able to school you on and let's turn the camera around on you. What are you going to discover? When are you going to lower your fear shield and not just advance physically, but also mentally?

When will you start expanding your mind and letting in thoughts that are truly originals? Are your political views your own or merely echoes from what others have told you or preached to you? Are your political opinions just regurgitated sound bites you've stolen from movies, TV and magazines? Have you ever really studied politics? Do you really know what you're talking about? Are you just following the pack, trying to fit in, be comfortable?

What about religion, art, culture? Do you really believe in God? Is Van Gogh's art really worth hundreds of millions versus the painting of a less well-known artist, or for that matter the scribblings of a monkey?

Hmmmmmmmm, I'm not bringing all these topics up to preach at you or make you feel insecure, I bring them up so that you can challenge yourself to know who you really are. So that you know your thoughts are just as valid as anyone else's. Don't let fear make you edit or readjust your thoughts. Let them be, let them thrive, let them live.

Let people move around your thoughts and be challenged by them. Remember, we only live once. Let your words move someone, even if it's only yourself. Let us learn from you. Why not?

DID YOU KNOW THAT SPEED BUMPS ARE JUST LAZY ROAD WORKERS?

We all hate speed bumps. They are probably one of the most annoying things in life. They slow us down, they scrape the underbellies of our cars, they're just no fun at all. I guess the upside of these annoying humps is that they protect neighborhoods from fast moving cars and cranked up teenagers who like to street race. But there is another side to these odd humps, a more sinister side.

Have you ever pulled to the side of the road, yanked a pickax out of your trunk and began excavating a speed bump? If you have a weak stomach and don't have a penance for horror movies I suggest you don't try it. Because encased in these so-called "speed bumps" are human remains.

Yup, I said it. Speed bumps are nothing more than asphalt sarcophagus's for lazy road workers. These bumps are nothing more than construction company employees who fell asleep on the job and simply got paved over.

You've seen the guy standing hour on end holding the little stop sign while the big road surfacing machines lay down fresh asphalt. Well, there is nothing more boring than standing in the blazing sun with a construction hat on and melting tar steaming in your face. It's enough to make anyone drowsy. So, unfortunately, many of these low paid workers drop to the ground to catch a few winks. Well, the man, he don't wait for nobody. The road has got to go through. And since most of the sign holders don't posses any other great skills it's easier to just pave over them and make a speed bump out of them. No one ever really reports them missing. If you don't believe me, pull out your pickax and start digging into a speed bump. You'll change your tune after you get down about two inches and you lay eyes on a human skeleton wearing a neon orange reflective vest.

DID YOU KNOW THAT GIRLS WITH COLAGEN LIPS ARE EXCELLENT FISH TANK CLEANERS?

Nothing is worse than the green scum that grows on the side of your fish tank. It is really difficult to get that stuff off. It's messy, grimy, and smelly. Thanks to the amazing world of cosmetic surgery there is now a solution, Collagen lips. Ahhhhh, the miracle cure. Now cleaning your fish tank is economical and easy.

By befriending a woman who has had this cosmetic procedure you, the fish tank owner, will be the beneficiary.

The process is economical because women pay for the costly procedure to have their lips puffed up, you don't pay a dime.

It's easy because all you need is a few glasses of cheap champagne to inebriate your collagen-lipped friend.

A drunk woman will do just about anything. Asking her to suck the algae off your forty-gallon fish tank is a no brainer. Sit back and marvel as she becomes a dirty human catfish. Kick your feet up and relax as she stuffs her head in the tank and her giant lips inch across the glass and suck the scum like a vacuum cleaner on shag.

Make sure they are careful not to suck up the snails, fish, or gravel. This could lead to intestinal trouble as well as gas. If satisfied with the fish tank, pour an extra glass of booze and encourage her to do all the windows in your house.

DID YOU KNOW THAT MAGIC MARKERS ARE NOT USED BY WIZARDS?

Much to contrary belief, magic markers are incapable of casting spells, making objects disappear or make cars float. They are not good to ride on. You cannot fly on a magic marker. Any wizard will tell you that all magic markers are good for is doodling and drawing colorful illustrations.

You will not be able to stop a troll or a demon in his tracks by waving a yellow "magic" marker at it. You will not be able to float or turn mice into dragons with a magic marker. They are primarily good for doing presentations, illustrating children's books, or sketching in art class. Do not attempt to turn a toad into a prince by tapping it three times with a Sharpie.

Just take your magic markers and go and draw a pretty landscape or a bird or the sun. Show the brightly colored drawing to your friends and enjoy the magic look on their faces as they see what a crappy artist you are.

DID YOU KNOW THAT NOSTRIL HAIRS CAN SAVE YOUR MARRIAGE?

Love is a very hard road to travel. We've all taken a ride on it. It has more ups and downs than a Motel 6 mattress. One of the most trying moments in a relationship is when the fighting begins. A bad fight can often lead to hurt and damaged feelings, and in some cases a total break up.

Men are often accused of not showing emotions. I guess you could say it is harder for us to cry. Not sure why it's just the way it is.

Sometimes showing emotion can be the only way to get back into your girls heart after a long and hurtful fight. Sadly, men often end up sleeping on the couch because the women don't believe men are sorry. That they aren't demonstrating the passion or the emotion that convinces them that the fight is over and that they are remorseful for even engaging in an altercation. A few shedded tears would make such a difference, if only men knew the secret to crying.

Well here it is. Next time you have a fight and it's obvious you are losing or you've had enough and just want it to end, here's what you do.

Pretend to get emotional, excuse yourself from the room and head into the bathroom. Find a pair of tweezers in the drawer and stick them up your nose. Start grabbing on to some delicate nose hairs and then rip them out with the tweezers as fast as you can. You may feel an unpleasant pinch, which is not so desirable, but there is an upside. Shortly after you pluck the nose hairs a strange reaction occurs. For some reason your eyes start to water and tears begin to slide down your face. It's perfect. After a few moments of ripping those nasal hairs out just sit back and watch the waterworks. Once your face looks sufficiently tear filled run back out to your girlfriend. The first thing she will say is, "Ohhhhh, baby, are you crying?" At that point you quietly nod your head "yes", and then, the fight is over. She thinks you have emotions. She thinks that you're sensitive and that you care.

You've got her right where you want her as she runs over and hugs you and cradles you in her breast. "Oh baby, I've never seen you get so emotional before, I'm sorry."

And it is at that point you say in a soft, broken voice, "So, do you think it would be okay for us to go down to Hooters and watch the hockey game on the flat screen now?" Without missing a beat she'll start kissing your salty tears away and say "Whatever you want baby, whatever you want." And then as she pays for all your beers and chicken wings she says, "I love you baby." And as you watch the hockey replay in slow motion you reply, "You too. I love you too."

DID YOU KNOW THAT INCHWORMS ARE USUALLY WELL OVER AN INCH?

Most inchworms are well over an inch long. Whoever named inchworms needs a new tape measure.

DID YOU KNOW THAT PEOPLE FROM GREENLAND HATE THE COLOR BLUE?

National pride can sometimes be a dangerous thing. People who get too passionate about their country can become pompous. An overabundance of pride in ones homeland can lead to fights, and in some cases all out war.

We all take great pride in our county of origin, it's almost something you can't turn off, but there is one country, Greenland, which has allowed their patriotism to ascend to a new low.

When your county's name has a color in its title you obviously develop a fondness for that particular color. Okay, that's fine, but, to not like other colors because of that? That is ignorant and almost racist in a way.

People in Greenland, or Greenlanders, hate the color blue. They don't want to hear about it, think about it or even see it. During the winter Greenlanders rejoice as their country is plunged into twenty-four hour darkness and they don't have to see the wretched blue color of the sky. Summer is the opposite with twenty-four hours of sunlight. It is this time of year that Greenlanders wear green tinted sunglasses and try to avoid looking at the sky or sea. It is truly a case of pure color snobbery.

The Greenlanders need to lower their shields of intolerance and allow the color blue into their daily existence. To not do so is to rob the eyes of one of our most beautiful colors. Greenland needs to open themselves up and stop the hating. I'm sure you all know why Frank Sinatra never preformed in Greenland? That's right, his eyes!

DID YOU KNOW THAT LOW INCOME FAMILY'S USE EGGO'S AS LEGGO'S?

Unfortunately not everyone is born with a silver spoon in his or her mouths. A sad reality of life is that many families struggle on a day-to-day basis in order to make ends meet. Sometimes money allocation has to struggle between eating, schooling, entertaining, and sometimes even toys for the children at Christmas. Believe it or not some children go without.

But now there is a new approach to this dilemma that kills two birds with one stone. Low-income parents have come up with an ingenious and practical solution to the toys vs. food problem. Parents have combined their children's toys with their food! They are now one and the same thing.

Low-income parents discovered that Eggo brand waffles and Leggo brand building blocks possess essentially the same letters in their name, Leggo of course having the extra 'L'. They also discovered that they are similar in appearance wherein Leggo's have a series of convex symmetrical protrusions, and Eggo's similarly have a series of concave symmetrical indentations. The outcome is the same, they are both great for constructing anything that may enter into a child's imaginative mind. The difference with the Eggo's is when a child finishes building an Eggo house or an Eggo castle, his mother can instruct him to butter it, add maple syrup, and then proceed to consume his creation. "You made your castle, now go ahead and eat it, Billy."

With Leggo's, tragically an opposite outcome occurs. Many children who have attempted to butter and eat the little red and green Leggo bricks, come face to face with disaster. There is a term familiar to toy manufacturers of the world that chills their blood 'CHOKING HAZZARD'.

Sadly many toddlers die after attempting to eat a gas station or spaceship built of Leggo. So, for those of you low income parents who borrowed this book and have not heard the good word, here it is. Treat your kid to Eggo's a wonderful, creative food/toy that he can eat for breakfast or at snack time. Your child will love them. Try the cinnamon swirl or blueberry flavors too!

DID YOU KNOW THAT LARRY SMITH IS AT THE END OF THE RAINBOW?

I've always been told that there is a pot of gold at the end of the rainbow. My whole life I've wanted to believe it. About two years ago I was looking to buy a new sports car, it wasn't going to be cheap. I was going to need some extra cash, a lot of it. I didn't want to take out a loan or borrow from friends or family and I certainly did not want to increase the hours on my workweek. I needed a viable solution. Something that would let me realize my dreams without putting me in debt.

One cloudy day, as I was staring out my window at the rain, feeling depressed about my situation, the clouds suddenly parted. The rain stopped abruptly and the golden sun came peering through the dreary grey clouds, sending them scurrying away. And as I felt the glow of the sun warm my face one of nature's most beautiful spectacles appeared before my eyes.

There in the brilliant blue sky, with the smell of a fresh spring rain hanging in the air, a rainbow arched across the sky in all its stunning brilliance. Reds, pinks, yellow's green's, blue, orange, and some purple too. It was breathtaking, as if God himself had reached from the heavens and made a brushstroke across the sky with a magic paintbrush. And as my eyes absorbed the majesty of this vision I had an epiphany.

I remembered that at the end of every rainbow lies an overflowing pot of shiny gold. My new sports car was as good as paid for. I threw on my tweed windbreaker and jumped in my old car. I followed the rainbow in eager anticipation knowing full well that this was probably one of the last times I'd be driving my Ford Focus. The rainbow stretched for miles, crossing the entire city, but I did not lose hope, I forged on anticipating the feel of gold bullion running through my fingers.

Only forty-five minutes later I was nearing the end of the rainbow. Miraculously it seemed to be touching down in a somewhat lower end neighborhood. Undeterred I kept going until at last I saw the rainbows end. It had landed right on the roof of a somewhat deteriorated house with an unmanicured lawn.

I heard an empty beer bottle crunch under my wheels as I parked the car at the curb and walked toward the front door of the house. My heart danced with glee as I could only imagine what was waiting for me on the other side of the door at number four twenty three Carbide Ave. Would my eyes be greeted with blinding magical light as the door opened? Would I be greeted by a cheery Irish leprechaun? My finger trembled as I pushed the cracked doorbell button. I stood nervously on the stained welcome matt that had the Jack Daniels logo on it. Suddenly my wait was over.

The door was opened. The first thing that hit me was the smell of stale food. My nostrils actually shut themselves. Next I was confronted by a slovenly man in a dirty undershirt and twisted boxer shorts. "Whatt'ya want?" he said as he took a bite out of a rather large dill pickle.

"I followed the rainbow!" I said with the excitement of a little schoolboy.

"Are you on meth, asshole?" He asked forcibly.

"No," I replied earnestly, "I'm here for the pot of gold. You are the gold's keeper aren't you?"

"No, I'm Larry Smith, I work for Frito Lay. I drive a forklift. Are you from the union?"

I stood there speechless, my dreams of a new BMW crashing to the ground as I stood in the reek of this unshaven man with a nibblet of corn hanging on his lower cheek.

"You wanna come in and watch some porn?" He quipped innocently.

As I struggled to hold back the tears, I could feel my lower lip quiver as I weakly responded. "No, not today thanks Larry." And without another word I returned to my Ford Focus and drove back toward home.

As I drove I naively started wondering if the wish I had made on the shooting star I saw last night would come true? Would Cher and Adrian Barbeau be waiting nude on my couch when I walked in my front door? Probably not.

DID YOU KNOW THAT HAIR PLUGS MAKE GREAT SHAG CARPETS?

Stepping out of bed in the morning can be a real drag, especially if your floors are bald. A carpetless floor means a cold floor and no one likes to walk across a cold floor. Carpeting is the obvious solution but carpets wear out and get dirty. What we need is something that can be washed and conditioned and smells good. We need to be able to style our carpets in this world of ever changing trends. A great way to do this is with hair plugs. Simply have your hardwood or concrete floors injected with thousands of tiny hair plugs.

Cover part of your floor or go all out and go wall to wall. Nothing will feel softer on your feet than silky human hair running through your toes in the morning. And you can change color to match your room. You could have blonde floors in the living room, chestnut brown in the bedroom, and curly, bouncy red just full of body in the den or family room.

No more hiring expensive and annoying carpet cleaners. Now you can just wash your rugs with Pert or strawberry scented VO-5 and then style them. Imagine a nice crimped den or a family room with braided floors. The possibilities are endless. With extra coarse hair you can make a great indoor-outdoor carpet for the hallway or entrance area and with extra thick hair a nice shag hair plug carpet always goes good in the game room.

Another bonus is the coloring options. With some L'Oreal you could tint your hair plug rugs, add highlights or change the color all together. How fun does a Brunette area rug become when suddenly it's strawberry blonde. Or how about getting creative, grabbing a few tubes of Revlon for Women and squirting patterns on your hair plug rug, voila', you now have a gorgeous Persian. For stains or areas where the hair may have fallen out, a simple box of Just for Men hair dye will fill in those damaged areas. Whatever you decide one thing is for sure, the next time you spill grape juice on your carpet you'll be having too much fun putting it in curlers and blow drying it to even get mad.

CHAPTER FOURTEEN

LET'S GET TECHNICAL!

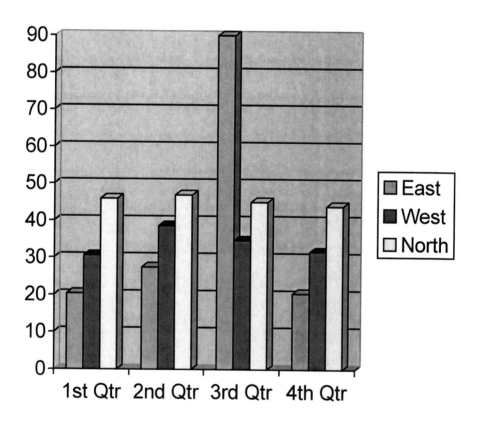

Before you do anything else I want you to look really closely at the graph on the preceding page. This is extremely important. Really take a moment to go over it. In particular check out the growth rate of the East in the third quarter. It is skyrocketing and has been propelled to an unbelievable ninety percent. This is almost unheard of. It far exceeds the stagnant and predictable rates of all activity in the first, second and fourth quarters. I find it incredible that all sectors lagged so far behind with none of them surpassing the fifty percent mark until the spike in the third quarter. Sixty and seventy percent is where you want to be. The West and the North both have a lot of work to do. With the East showing such dominance in the third quarter it will be very hard for West and North to recover when the next cycle begins. How do you feel about my assessment? Do you agree or disagree??

So? What do you think? Confused? Well, you should be. Everything I just said has no meaning. The graph is in reference to absolutely nothing, but because it was a 'GRAPH' you gave it credibility. Maybe that's what's stopping you from having pure and inventive thoughts. Maybe you've trained your brain to be too technical. To place too much importance on structure and logic. Look at that chart again, isn't it the most boring thing you've ever seen? But this is the way much of society has trained us to see the world. Everything does not have to be so academic and linear. What would you rather watch, the movement of this graph or a jellyfish moving gracefully behind the glass of an aquarium? Which one would stimulate you more? Which would spark your imagination, your wonderment? Which would make you marvel, appreciate beauty, inspire you to ask questions? I won't say what's right or wrong because for all I know a graph holds the beauty of a jelly fish, but either way don't let your mind become as technical as a graph. In fact too much technical intake can step on your spiritualness. I'm not talking god or heaven or hell, I'm just talking about your demeanor, your ability to be lighthearted, to open up, let down your guard and laugh, smile, be amused by the little things... a jellyfish. In fact here's an exercise that might help you technically wired individuals loosen your collars.

Next time you look at a graph like the one on the preceeding page I want you to imagine how much time in your life you have dedicated to all the technical stuff you were trained and programmed to pay attention to. Now I want you to hold that up against how much time you've spent allowing your mind to run and create its own ideas. So, now looking at the graph change the meaning of it. Don't look at it as profits or growth or volumes or commodities, look at it like it's a heart monitor. You know the ones you always see in the ER and they beep along to your heartbeat. Now, look at that huge spike in the third quarter and imagine that that spike is your massive heart attack and your life flashed before your eyes. Do you continue into the fourth quarter with business as usual or do you make a change? Do you look at your life and say "Did I let my brain really think for itself or did it get programmed by society the day they gave me a social security number at birth? Hmmmmmmm… Did you know that as long as you are alive it's never too late to think!

DID YOU KNOW THAT DRIVING DOWN THE INFORMATION SUPERHIGHWAY COULD DAMAGE YOUR COMPUTER?

Society has an insatiable appetite for information. It is estimated that people spend more time on their computers than they do watching television. The term used to encapsulate all the computer data is 'The Information Superhighway'. It pretty much sums it up.

Computers are so inundated with activity that they need a metaphorical highway to put everyone on. The highway has many exit ramps and seems to go on for infinity. The one piece of information that is not included on the information superhighway is this; you cannot actually drive your vehicle down the information superhighway. A few weeks ago I was feeling the urge to go on a road trip. I was looking for somewhere new and exciting. I wanted to see things I hadn't seen before. I made the mistake of choosing the information superhighway.

At exactly 9:00am last Tuesday morning I loaded up my Dodge Ram pickup truck, put it in drive and tried to drive into my laptop computer that I had placed, sitting open on my driveway.

I was incredibly excited about going down a highway I had never been. What possibilities await me? What scenery? What adventure. Well, it didn't take long for my road trip to get derailed. As I drove into my laptop I heard a sickening *CRUNCH!!* The unmistakable sound of rubber wheel meeting aluminum casing. I could feel the technology of my computer crunching under my tires like the bones of a wary raccoon that mistimed his crossing of a busy road. My laptop was completely demolished, I had failed to even complete the first inches of a mile on the information superhighway.

So, for the benefit of those, who like me, weren't aware that the information superhighway is closed to all vehicles, now you know. Next time I want access I'll just log on and let my fingers do the driving. Until then, I'll be busy planning my next road trip. Think I'll go to the desert.

DID YOU KNOW THAT CELLULITE MAKES FOR GREAT STORAGE SPACE?

The dreaded 'C' word! Cellulite! Nobody likes it or wants it. The faintest trace of it can send a woman into fits of depression, outrage, and panic. The unsightly divots in the back of the legs, thighs, and buttocks are not pleasant to look at. Caused by water retention and hardening of the skins connective tissue, cellulite can effect anyone, not just the obese.

So how do we put a positive spin on such an unwanted and socially scorned affliction? Does the term "Hey, has anyone seen my car keys?" ring a bell? You bet it does. We are always losing our keys, or can't find enough coins for the parking meter, or have nowhere to put hairpins, lipstick, cell phones or even a small snack like a cookie or some raisins. Well cellulite sufferers rejoice.

That dimpled cottage cheese you wear on your skin is no longer a negative, but now, a valuable asset. We as humans are like pack rats, always looking for more space to store things. There never seems to be enough room. Well, now there is. It's those three-inch welts on your lower body, yes, your cellulite.

The fleshy depressions you have grown are perfect little nooks to place car keys and trinkets. You need never have to wonder again about where you left your keys. They'll always be right there nestled in that fleshy little crevasse just below your left buttock. And how about not having time to grab a snack during the day? You're working hard, you're tired, you can't get out of a meeting and your stomach is grumbling. No problem. Just nonchalantly reach down the back of your pants or skirt and pull the chocolate chip cookie out that's been stored in the cellulite meat cave on your ass. Some cellulite welts get so big they could even be used for bigger items such as iPod's or small pets. Maybe from here on out we can look at cellulite as a blessing and not a curse. Embrace our washboard jelly welts and make them work for us and not against us.

DID YOU KNOW THAT DONUTS CAN HELP YOU SLEEP?

Lying in bed wide-awake is horrible. Insomnia is an affliction that nobody likes. It's almost akin to being tortured. You toss and turn and no matter what you do you just can't seem to doze off. Well, thank thee good lord that many donut shops are open twenty-four hours, because they might just hold the answer to that peaceful night sleep you so crave. The next time you can't sleep don't go for pills or medicines, warm milk or counting sheep, try this. Jump in the car and speed to a convenient Dunkin Donuts. Purchase two honey-glazed donuts and speed home. After exiting your car, carefully place the honey-glazed donuts on your eyes. Don't worry, the sugary glaze coating will help them stick to your face. Once the donuts are in place locate a large pine tree or any other species of tree you can find. Climb the tree slowly and find a thick branch that can support your weight. Sit on the branch, get comfortable, and start pretending you're an owl.

With the donuts on your eyes you already have the perfect look. Start 'whooooing' just the way an owl would. Continue this for a half hour to an hour. Eventually you will start to tire and most likely nod off and fall from the tree.

Upon impact with the ground below, if all goes well, you will be knocked unconscious instantly, and in essence will be completely asleep. Depending on the severity of the fall and the force of the impact, your slumber time will vary with each session. Even more fantastic is when your eyes finally flutter open in your driveway or on your lawn, you will have a bonus treat waiting on your face. Most of us when we first wake up like to head straight for the kitchen for a morning snack. Well, imagine waking up and finding a delicious snack right on your face? Two delectable honey glazed donuts resting on your eyes. It really doesn't get any better.

DID YOU KNOW THAT YOU'RE A LIVING CONNECT THE DOTS?

One of anyone's fondest childhood memories has to be our very first 'connect the dots' book. Remember the enchantment, the magic of taking a pencil and connecting the dots? Never knowing what an image would be until it at last came to light by the power of your hand. Would it be a bird, a fire truck, a monster? Who knew? The mystery could only be solved by you.

As we all grew older a void begins to manifest in our lives. The innocence and wonderment of youth seems to have long slipped away. It can be hard in a fast paced world to reconnect with our past, with our innocence, with our childhood. Any good psychologist can tell you that retaining your childlike spirit is a healthy part of your development as a human being.

So what can one do to go back in time and experience our wonderful youth? You don't have to go back in time. All you need to do is go to a handy bathroom and take off all your clothes!

Now wait a second, don't get ahead of yourselves, this is not some creepy kind of deviant behavior thing, this is honest to goodness reconnecting to yourself by actually connecting. Connecting the dots!

Grab a Sharpie magic marker and go to the nearest bathroom, at home, the office, a train station, wherever you may be. Pull off all your clothes and stand in front of a mirror. And don't worry about the sneers and baffled looks of people in public restrooms, they are just acting like adults.

Now, take in your body in your reflection. Absorb the nudity and study it. Turn and bend, lift and separate, do whatever you have to do to locate all the freckles on your body. Big ones small ones, whatever. Next, uncap the Sharpie and place the tip on your skin at the first desired freckle. From there draw a black line to the next freckle, and then the next one. Do you see where this is going?

Yes, that's right, your face is probably beaming with delight at this point as you realize you have truly stepped back in time and are now connecting the dots. The dots on your naked body!

What surprise will your body unfold? What are the secrets of your freckles? Have you been hiding a rocket ship all these years? A giant apple, a dinosaur? Only you can find the answer by connecting your freckles.

I did mine a few weeks ago and imagine my surprise when I realized I had an image of Michael Landon riding a dune buggy, on my back.

And should you run out of freckles the good news is you can always lay in the sun hours upon end and create new freckles, some of them even quite big and sometimes changing shape. Let's get back to being kids. Connect with your inner child, connect with your freckles.

DID YOU KNOW NERDS MAKE GREAT COLE SLAW?

Summertime treats are always delish. Summer isn't summer without a picnic or a BBQ, and one of the staples at these fun filled events is delicious, fresh, coleslaw. Mmmmmmmmm! Yummmmm! And on the same note, nothing can ruin a picnic faster then someone yelling, "We forgot the coleslaw!" What a downer. People can still pretend to have a good time but we all know, no slaw = no guffaw.

Enter the freckled faced nerd kid with the red hair and the huckleberry hound t-shirt. There's always one nerd kid in the crowd at every summertime, outdoor event, and where there's nerd kids, there's braces. I'm not talking leg braces I'm talking teeth braces. Good old-fashioned metal train tracks. These are an invaluable tool when the presence of coleslaw is in doubt.

In order to make sure there is enough yummy slaw for everybody, here is the procedure. Grab a fresh head or two of cabbage from anybody's cooler or picnic basket. Hold it firmly in one hand. Locate the freckled faced nerd kid with the braces. Grab him by the tuft of his hair on the back of his head. Instruct him to smile broadly, making sure he is fully exposing his shiny, metal braces. Bring the cabbage to his mouth and start grinding it back and forth in a vigorous horizontal motion.

The nerd may protest and try to wriggle free at first, but maintain enough force and rhythmic motion to keep the kids mouth moving like a cheese grater. Within seconds shreds of cabbage will begin falling from the nerds mouth and into a large bowl placed under his chin. Use as many cabbages as needed to fill the bowl. Ensure there is enough coleslaw for all to enjoy. The nerd may experience some mild humiliation as well as possible bleeding of the gums. But, that is a small price to pay in order to save a fun time, summer event.

DID YOU KNOW WOMEN BREAST FEED TECHNOLOGY?

People love their technology, even to the point where they give their cell phones names or refer to them as their babies. So it should come as no surprise to see women opening their shirts in public places and breast-feeding their "babies?" Holding iPhones over their nipples and encouraging them to suckle.

It is scary the way humans have begun to personalize their technology.

Breast-feeding phones is only going to lead to false dreams of motherhood and could spill into post partum depression. Women must be careful that their mothering instincts do not lure them into an imagined reality where impossible mother/ child relationships can never exist. And on top of all that, some of the corrosive enzymes in breast milk could potentially cause irreparable damage to your phone.

DID YOU KNOW THAT ZYXT IS THE LAST WORD IN THE ENGLISH DICTIONARY?

I would think so. I mean look at it. Zyxt is one ugly ass word. I'm not even going to tell you what it means, it's not worth it. It's a word you will never ever, ever use in your lifetime. That's probably why they stuck it at the back of the book. Who wants it? What an ugly duckling indeed.

As far as words go it is a *LOOOOSSSSSER!* It almost looks like someone shook up a bag of Scrabble letters and dumped them on a table and said, "There! That right there is a word, zyxt!" What a joke.

At least the first word in the dictionary is something we can understand, 'Aardvark', we all know this loveable little fellah! Cute little ground dwelling anteater type of guy. Sure, why not kick the English language off with a cuddly little character? Can you think of a more settling and loveable way to begin a language? I mean if baby seal was a word and started with three a's then maybe, aaababyseal? Sure that could be cute, but aardvark is still a winner.

In stark comparison zyxt can go straight to hell. In fact it sounds like something Satan himself would say. He probably uses it as an under his breath curse mumble. Can you picture the lord of darkness seated on his flaming throne, one of his minions approaches, "Dear Satan, dark master of the unholy underworld, I know today was supposed to be a day off for you my liege, but a whole new load of souls has just come in from above."

And then knowing his "day off" plans are ruined, the devil mumbles under his breath "zyxt...."

"I beg your pardon? What was that my lord?"

"Nothing, get out of here before I lose my temper."

I propose that zebra become the last word in the dictionary. We started the language off with an adorable mammal and we should end the language with an adorable mammal. If zyxt insists on being the last word then lets rename baby rabbits. A baby rabbit would be known as a zyxt! It doesn't get much cuter than that.

DID YOU KNOW I'M WATCHING YOU RIGHT NOW?

I know it sounds creepy but it's true. I know you all know about Google, right? It's a search engine that has a ton of incredible applications. It supplies us with almost all the knowledge you will ever need, with the exception of course of what this book has taught you. And of course, the original thoughts you are going to conjure up in the fabulous years ahead.

One of the features Google has is one that is allowing me to watch you right now, it's called Google Earth. Basically it's a satellite that allows me to look at the planet from orbit and zoom in on anyone, anywhere, anytime. I may be watching you right now reading my vunderbar book! I hope you are enjoying it. Or should I say enjoyed it? Alas, you are now on the final pages. It's not that I ran out of things to tell you it's just that I want to dole it out in portions, like a fine meal.

My wish is that this book informed you but at the same time opened the garage door in your mind and will give you the courage to allow yourself to have your own ideas. To think on your own terms. To put your mind out there for people to see, interpret and enjoy. Godspeed, and may your brain take you to all the nooks and crannies of your mind. English muffin!

P.S. The guy in the purple t-shirt and grey sweats, reading outside the Starbucks on Ventura, stop picking your nose.

LET'S CLOSE IT UP!

IT'S TIME TO GO NOW MY FRIENDS!

DID YOU KNOW THAT THIS BOOK IS NOT REALLY OVER?

For two reasons this book is not over.

1. I want this book to be the starting off point for you to keep searching for all the things you didn't know. So if anything you read inspires you, then you are keeping the book alive.

2. There has to be a blooper reel, right? Sure, they're always fun. So, the following is a list of words I spelled wrong and a couple of sentences where I totally used the wrong grammar.

WORD BLOOPERS:

- Restaurant
- Tongue
- Field
- Terrestrial
- Biometrics
- zimmazoomazingagong
- a
- potatoe skins

SENTENCE BLUNDERS:

- I decided to go to the pubic library.
- Sometimes even I know not stuff like.
- And the Indian threw a fit of epilepsy, cupcake.
- It's very important that the st;ore stay open.
- Sourdough bread is yummy't.

I hope you enjoyed these hilarious outtakes. Until next time my friends…. Did you know that this is….

THE END

CPSIA information can be obtained at www.ICGtesting.com
Printed in the USA
LVOW11s1951231214

420102LV00001B/94/P